The Abingdon Religious Education Texts
John W. Langdale, General Editor
COMMUNITY TRAINING SCHOOL SERIES. NORMAN E. RICHARDSON, Editor

Religious Education
Through Story-Telling

BY
KATHERINE D. CATHER

THE ABINGDON PRESS
NEW YORK   CINCINNATI   CHICAGO

CONTENTS

EDITOR'S INTRODUCTION

THE developments taking place in the field of religious education have created a demand for a new study of method in teaching religion. Teachers and supervisors are asking, "How does the pupil experience religion?" It is the steps in this process that suggest the mode of procedure in teaching. Method is not determined by the nature of the lesson materials alone. It grows out of the processes whereby the pupil learns to live the Christian life. To facilitate this process is the function of method. Improvement in method will come through clearer insight into the natural ways by which children come to an experience of religion.

With a clearer understanding of how children and young people learn to live this Christian life there comes a more intelligent and enthusiastic appreciation of the story as a means of religious education. Stories that are properly selected and well told quicken latent energies, help to set up channels of energy release, and provide action patterns to guide this energy, bringing it to desirable points of expression. The emotionalized mental furnishings of the pupil are organized around and identified with ethical ideals. Desirable forms of religious experience are set up within the pupil's life. And all this takes place without compromising the spontaneity and naturalness of the child's mode of procedure in learning.

In preparing the present volume, Katherine D.

Cather brings to her task a wide and intelligent familiarity with the world's best story literature and what it has done in building our present world civilization. She is a seasoned master of the art of story-telling. Her insight into the spontaneous interests, needs, and limitations of child life is easily apparent. Though many books on this subject have appeared, it is safe to say that none equal the present volume in bringing to teachers the practical help they need in mastering the art of story-telling. The material has been carefully adapted to the requirements of the standard training course of the International Council of Religious Education. No one studying its chapters can fail to catch some of the author's enthusiasm and conviction concerning the value of story-telling as a means of helping children to come into desirable forms of Christian experience.

NORMAN E. RICHARDSON.

CHAPTER I

THE UNIVERSAL APPEAL OF THE STORY

MANY centuries ago there was a banquet in Bagdad, given by a caliph who rejoiced in the birth of a son. Every man of high station in the capital partook of the feast, and each one brought a costly gift for the babe—each except a young sage named Mehelled Abi. He came empty-handed.

"Fine raiment, jewels, and gold the prince will receive in rich store," this portionless guest exclaimed as he salaamed to the caliph in greeting. "Therefore he shall have from me something more precious than any of these. Each day of his life, from the time he is old enough to understand until he enters the gate of manhood, I will tell him stories that will make him both wise and righteous. And when thy days are done in Bagdad, O Caliph, and he sits above the people as their chief, he will be just and merciful, a ruler in whom all Arabia will rejoice."

Mehelled Abi kept his word. As soon as the child, who was named Haroun-al-Raschid, could speak and understand, a dark-robed figure came to the palace and recounted stories that embodied all that was best in Arabian history and thought. Not for a few months, or a few years came he, but throughout the prince's boyhood and youth. When finally Haroun became caliph, the fame of his good works spread throughout the east. Then his teacher inscribed on a scroll that is still to be seen in the Lichtenthal collection of manuscripts at Budapest, "It was because of the seed sown by the tales."

Those who have studied the history of story-telling, and who have watched the results of purposeful, systematic oral narration among children to-day, believe Mehelled Abi was not mistaken in his contention. Carefully planned, artistic story-telling by one whose heart is in the work, and who believes in the power of the story, can achieve results that are almost past believing. It *is* achieving such results to-day in centers in the great American cities where gather children who are the problem and opportunity of social service workers.

It has been achieving them throughout the ages. Story-telling has ever been a medium of culture, a teacher of history, literature, and ethics. It has instilled religious thought and feeling, in both children and adults. It has been a maker of standards and builder of ideals, not only in one century or country, but during every age and in every land whose achievements have been chronicled.

The Use of Stories During Antiquity

When Socrates instructed the youth of Athens beneath the oleanders of old Greece, he emphasized to them through concrete example the principles he wished them to absorb. He told stories the characters of which were rewarded with peace of spirit and satisfaction in life through having made those principles their guide of conduct, or were denied the happiness that might have been theirs because of failure to heed them. Dialogue was the favorite form of expression, of this Hellenic sage.   Colloquy was used in which several characters argued their points and adjusted their differences. These dialogues, however, were enlivened in many places with bits of narrative introduced to drive theories home.

Plato, the great pupil of Socrates, adopted a like method.   Throughout his dialogues were scattered tales intended to fix in the minds and hearts of his followers the principles he advocated.   In his works that have come down to us are numerous narrative portions, some of them not more than a paragraph in length, but stories nevertheless, short, concise tales in which something happens that tends to awaken interest and establish belief.

In his *Phædrus*[1] we find the following illustration used as an argument against egotism, pretense, and desire to achieve without effort:

"In the neighborhood of Naucratis, in Egypt, there lived one of the ancient gods of that country whose name was Theuth. He was the first to invent numbers and arithmetic, geometry and astronomy, draughts, and above all, letters.   Now, the whole of Egypt at that time was under the sway of the god Thamus, who resided near the capital city of the upper region, which the Greeks call Thebes.   To him therefore Theuth repaired, and, displaying his inventions, recommended their general diffusion among the Egyptians.   Thamus asked him the use of each, and received his explanations, as he thought them good or bad, with praise or censure.

"Now, on each of the arts the god is reported

[1] The Phædrus, Lysis, and Protagoras of Plato, page 103. The Macmillan Company.   Used by permission.

to have said a great deal to Theuth, both in favor and disfavor. It would take a long story to repeat it all. But when they came to the letters, Theuth began, 'This invention, O king, will make the Egyptians wiser and better able to remember, it being a medicine which I have discovered for both memory and wisdom.'

"The king replied: 'Most ingenious Theuth, this invention of yours will produce a forgetfulness in the minds of those who learn it, by causing them to neglect their memory, inasmuch as from confidence in writing they will recollect by the external use of foreign symbols, and not by the internal use of their own faculties. You are providing for your disciples a show of wisdom without the reality. By it they will appear to possess much knowledge, while, in fact, they will know nothing at all. Moreover, they will be disagreeable people to deal with, as having become wise in their own conceit, instead of truly wise.' "

Plato introduced embryo stories into his dialogues for the same reason Socrates used them. He knew that the concrete grips and molds. He understood that through seeing his theories in action, through observing virtue or vice in living human beings, he could impress truths upon the minds and hearts of his pupils more deeply and lastingly than in any other way. Experience had taught him that truth presented in formal precept is often not comprehended. Even when comprehended it sometimes does not appeal. Therefore he made free use of a medium through which he had found it possible to make truth clear, and to make it attractive as well.

"In order to teach a child truth," this wise Athenian used to say, "it is necessary to teach him fiction."

He meant that before people can be sufficiently swayed by a truth or principle to make it the guiding rule of conduct it is necessary for them to see that principle in action. It is necessary for them to observe men suffering or rewarded according to their allegiance to some great precept. Through the play of imagination which the story gives, such observation and insight are possible.

The use of stories by Confucius.—Centuries before the days of Socrates and Plato there was a man in China who was fully appreciative of the wisdom of using stories in teaching religion and morality. His name was Confucius. In his youth he was but a keeper of herds for the chief of the district in which he lived, and he spent his early years in poverty. Yet he grew to be one of the greatest teachers and lawgivers of all time. He proclaimed to his people a better code of action than the one by which they had been governed from remote ages. He believed that morality and righteousness cannot be achieved from without, but come only through desire from within. He used stories to arouse desire for better conduct, because he discovered that in listening to accounts of those who had known the satisfaction of high conduct came desire to emulate them.

The use of stories by Christ and among the Hebrews.—When the Greatest Teacher of all began his work in Palestine he employed the story freely to illustrate principles and demonstrate truths. Through the parable of the good Samaritan he

taught the beauty of being merciful in a way that
unnumbered "Thou shalts" could not have done.
The parable of the sower, the parable of the fig
tree, the parable of the vineyard, the parable of the
lost coin and all the others are tales told to establish beliefs and awaken desire.   Never in the history
of the world has narrative been more freely drawn
upon to teach lessons than by Jesus of Nazareth.
He understood its power over the human heart, and
throughout his ministry employed it in his work.

As it was with Jesus, so it was with those who
preceded him as the teachers of the Israelites.
Like eager children were the men and women to
whom the Hebrew leaders spoke of the deeds of
outstanding figures of their race, of their heeding
or disobeying the voice of God and the reward or
punishment that came accordingly.   And because
the story has power to touch the heart as well as the
intellect the lessons given in this way were not
forgotten.

**The use of stories in Europe during the Dark
Ages.**—The period the world knows as the Dark
Ages was not wholly devoid of light and progress
because, during that time, there were many splendid
teachers in Europe.   Most of them are unsung
men as far as we are concerned, for only in a few
cases have their names come down to us, yet they
did an immortal work, and they did it largely
through the medium of oral narration.

There were two groups of these leaders.   One
was made up of missionaries who went from Italy,
where already Christianity had taken root, into
lands beyond the Alps whose inhabitants were
yet barbarians.   The other consisted of tribesmen

who recounted the traditions of their people to the rising generation. The missionaries preached the gospel to the clans of Gaul and Britain by telling of rewards enjoyed by those who had embraced the principles of Jesus—rewards that could not come to followers of the Druid god, Beltane. Their methods were the methods of Confucius, of Plato, of Jesus, of all, in fact, who have been the great religious mentors of the world.

Influence of the missionaries among the tribesmen.—Some of the missionaries who crossed the Alps had great influence with the western tribal leaders even before they succeeded in converting them to Christianity. Old chronicles make frequent mention of barbarian chiefs and sovereigns consulting these men in secular matters. The Italian bishop Remi was the counselor of the young Frankish king Clovis even while that impulsive and fiery monarch scoffed at his tales of acts of the Christian God. Yet by those same tales was Clovis swayed in a way that mystified him, and very often, because of their admonition, he modified his course of conduct, although he clung tenaciously to his heathen gods. Remi it was whom the Frank consulted when he wanted to take a bride who would be a credit to the Merovingian line and a joy to himself, and Remi wisely guided him to Clotilda of Burgundy, King Chilperic's young daughter, who, of all maids the Italian had met in Gaul, had taken deepest hold on his affections. She was little more than a child when he went to the Burgundian court in the hope of establishing the Christian faith there, but she listened to his words like one entranced. His tales of the Babe in the manger who became the Man of Sorrows, and the early Christian martyrs, were as food to her spirit. She embraced Christianity and never swerved in her allegiance to it. After her marriage to Clovis she labored hand in hand with the missionary to Christianize her husband and Gaul. After a labor of almost five years she succeeded.

Examples paralleling that of Remi can be cited from Britain, from Belgium, and from lands east of the Rhine where men worked in the same way as the Italian to establish the Christian faith, and by his methods achieved the same results. Every missionary who labored during the early Christian era presented principles through scattered bits of narrative instead of trying to teach them as abstract statements and axioms.

By the time of the ascension of Charlemagne, Christianity had become firmly established in western Europe. Yet many men still labored there to keep the flame of the faith burning at full intensity, and in order to do it they told and retold the tales which Bishop Remi and his colleagues had brought from the east. The outstanding churchman of Charlemagne's time was Turpin, Archbishop of Rheims, and numerous legends from that period acclaim him as a prince of story-tellers. No one could bring tears to the eyes and high resolve to the heart as could Turpin as he recounted narratives of Christ and the apostles. By the powerful emotional appeal of his tales he kept zeal for Christianity burning at a feverish pitch in Gaul, although he himself was doer of many an evil deed.

The use of stories by Buddah, Mohammed, and other religious teachers.—Buddah, "the Enlight-

ened," used the story in his teachings as freely as
Jesus used it.   He lived a recluse among the groves
of Bernares, struggling to overcome within himself
all that seemed unrighteous, and seeking for the
truth.   Then he went into the world and gave the
account of his experiences.   By his preaching and
tales he won millions to his faith.   The power of
Buddah in China, Japan, and India even now is
a monument to the lasting effectiveness of his method
of teaching.

Mohammed, prophet of the Moslems, spread his
gospel with fire and sword, and commanded his
followers to do likewise.   But he depended on something mightier than a blade of steel to perpetuate
his principles.   Whenever he was not fighting he
was picturing to his apostles the bliss that awaited
all believers in his doctrines, picturing to them the
beauty of the houris and the peri, the asphodel
meadows, the beguiling music, the days of ease and
nights of pleasure in the Paradise of the Koran.
It is the traditions of Mohammedanism, told and
retold for centuries at Saracenic firesides, that have
kept the Moslem faith alive in the world.

It was the same among the Scandinavians.
Christianity became the legalized religion of Norway in the early part of the eighth century, but
for a long time after that it was not the faith to
which the vikings turned in time of trouble.   The
power of the ancient tales still held them, and
although a Christianized king commanded their
attendance at Christian churches, while at home,
on the sea, in times of storm and danger, they
worshipped Thor.   To this day in isolated parts of
the island of Sicily, yearly religious observances are

conducted that are a survival of pagan times. The beliefs upon which they are founded never have been a part of the Catholic creed. For several centuries both church and state have united in an effort to eradicate these pagan observances. But because the stories that keep alive these beliefs are told by the old generation to the young, the people still cling to them. They believe as their fathers believed before them. It is by the lips of the story-teller that these beliefs have been kept alive.

Stories the first medium of systematic education. —Charlemagne, "the great emperor," who came to the throne of the Franks in 771, was a ruler of wider vision than any of his predecessors. He saw that in order to make his realm the power of which he dreamed he must be surrounded by men of valor. Bravery could be inculcated into youth by making them familiar with the high deeds of men of the past, so he set about finding teachers to undertake the instruction of boys of the blood-royal. He established at Paris schools in which history was taught. There being no books at that time save chronicles on rolls of parchment that were brought at great cost from the east, history was taught entirely by word of mouth. The teacher told stories of heroes of an earlier day, not only of Gaul, but of Italy, Greece, and the Orient. The education of a boy began at the age of ten and lasted throughout four or five years. Such instruction, it was believed, would equip him with knowledge and desire for high achievement that would greatly increase the quality of his knighthood.

The schools established by Charlemagne hardly

deserve the name when compared with those of our day, but as time passed they grew in number and improved. To the teaching of history and religion was added mathematics. Several centuries after the death of the great emperor the "royal schools" were united into an institution that later became the University of Paris.

Only boys of highest rank were received into the schools which Charlemagne established at Paris. But there were many youths among the lower nobility, and the emperor saw the wisdom of having them also versed in the lore of the past. "The more they know of heroes the more of heroes they will become," he often said. Consequently, he made provision for their education. He ordered men to go from castle to castle and tell stories of heroes of bygone times. Being a man of tremendous egotism, he commanded them to tell also of his own achievements, many of which were greatly exaggerated in the tales. Some of the feats attributed to him had no foundation whatever, but coming from the lips of the story-teller they were believed by lads who heard them. Not only were they believed, but perpetuated, passed on to a younger generation by those who had received them in youth. With the passing of centuries they became the great mass of Charlemagne legends that have come down to us.

Story-telling a part of minstrelsy.—As musical instruments were introduced into the world west of the Bosporus, strolling teachers whose business it was to recount the deeds of heroes often gave their tales with a lute or lyre accompaniment. This was the beginning of minstrelsy in Europe.

Music reached a high state of development in Greece, and musical instruments introduced from Persia, Arabia, and Egypt were much employed as an accompaniment to singing. From Greece the lyre, harp, and lute were taken to Italy, where they became very popular. Then they were carried beyond the Alps. But their use was confined to the Frankish dominions, and to Ireland, where the harp was known from very remote times. Probably the throbbing instrument the world has so long associated with the Emerald Isle was taken there by the Romans at the time of Cæsar's northward dash, and adopted by tribes still as primitive as any in the west, but more musically inclined than most of the others. At any rate, when Saint Patrick first visited Ireland, almost fifteen hundred years ago, he found the harp there. So far as we know, it was in use among the Irish people earlier than anywhere else in western Europe, although its origin in that land is a matter of conjecture.

Toward the end of the Dark Ages the harp had become part of the life of every country of central and western Europe. Wherever this instrument was known there were strolling bards who were the castle entertainers. With their songs and stories they furnished amusement and helped to give variety to a life that was confined within narrow boundaries. These bards were far more than entertainers. They were the historians of their age, who gave to the young the lore of the old. All the stories of great men and great deeds they gave with a harp accompaniment, because they understood the power of music over the emotions, and while song and tale were harmoniously blended the minstrel knew that he held his hearers in the hollow of his hand. In different lands these men were known by different names. In Britain and Ireland they were called minstrels; in Germany, minnesingers, and in France, trouvères, or troubadours. But always they were teachers, men with a mission and a message. Not until the beginning of modern times was history taught in any other way than by the lips of the story-teller.

Story-telling a method of instruction in Colonial times.—The ancient method of instruction was not wholly abandoned even after books came to be widely used. Numerous records show that as late as two centuries ago, in universities throughout Europe, but one book of history was used by a class. This was in the hands of the teacher, and from it he read and told stories. At the beginning of the Revolutionary War numerous history classes in the American colonies were conducted in this way.

THE INHERENT APPEAL OF THE STORY

Human emotions are fundamentally the same in every country and in every period of history, regardless of the degree of culture or the color of the skin. Love and hate lie dormant in the human heart; likewise gratitude, and all the other feelings that move mortals to action. They manifest themselves according to the state of civilization or enlightenment of those in whose souls they surge, but the elemental urge, the motive that actuates men to right or wrong doing, is the same now as it was at the beginning of time. The story has power to nurture any one of the emotions, because, when the child—even the adult whose code of belief is not firmly fixed—hears tales in which any of the base emotions are glorified, he comes to glorify them himself, or at least to justify them. People reared in lands whose national heroes are fierce, avenging heroes grow into men of fierceness. To them a show of mercy is a badge of weakness. Pity is something of which a strong man should be ashamed. Odin and Thor, of the ancient Norse mythology, were merciless, terrible gods, and because of the belief of the people in them the ancient code of the north-land was a terrible code. According to it, robbery and murder were justifiable and honorable, so long as they were perpetrated upon strangers, or beyond the boundaries of one's own land. Consequently, from the fjords of Norway came the vikings, pillaging and plundering along the shores of foreign lands. Not until after the Scandinavian people yielded to the softening influence of Christianity, not until heroes of gentleness and mercy supplanted the gods of violence of the old tales, were the ancient, fierce laws revoked in the north. Because the story of Mohammed is still the sacred narrative of the Moslems, massacres of Christians have been perpetrated by the Turks even in our own time. The Prophet taught his followers that it is justifiable and holy to spread the faith with fire and sword, that whoever kills an unbeliever is pleasing in the eyes of Allah. Therefore both spahis and foot soldiers massacre with fanatical zeal, believing that in wiping out opponents of their religion they are doing right.

The story touches the heart.—Examples from almost every land can be cited as evidence of the influence the frequently retold story has had upon human action. As one thinks upon the subject, the question arises, Why? What is the secret of the power of either the spoken or written tale to shape ideals and fix standards? Because it touches the heart. It arouses the emotions and makes people *feel* with the characters whose acts make the plot. Mirth, anger, pity, desire, disdain, approval, and dislike are aroused, because the characters who move through the tale experience these emotions. In listening to a story one is moved to pity by the misfortunes of his fellows and rejoices in their happiness and success. Dislike for a person who perpetrates a wrong upon another is aroused in hearing an account of an act of injustice. Approval of him who is merciful to the unfortunate is aroused to an equal pitch by a narrative portraying kindliness. For the moment the listener forgets himself and experiences, thinks and feels with the hero of the story. This hero may be a person of another land or another race, but he is a human being. He knows sorrow, or happiness. He is brave or cowardly, and the emotions that are common to all human kind are called into play in seeing him move through a tale.

The story feeds the desire for experience.— There is no age and no temperament to which the narrative does not appeal because it feeds the desire for experience that characterizes every human being. From the beginning until the end of life people are interested in the experiences of others. In hearing about the activities of others one is vicariously widening the range of his own experience. The same instinct that impels a person to listen eagerly to stories underlies fondness for hearing gossip or scandal. Whether worthy or unworthy tales are being told, the curtain is for the moment drawn aside from the lives of others. To the casual observer the skilled narrator seems to have almost hypnotic power, so completely do his hearers fall under the sway of his words while listening to a tale. But the secret of his power is in his ability to make the characters of the story so alive and human that those who hear it live with them and enter into their experiences.

The story is a tool of universal adaptability.— Because the story has power to awaken the emotions and to enlarge the range of experience, it is a tool of universal adaptability. Its appeal is like that of music, sculpture, or painting. The old and the young alike are swayed by it, the cultured and the illiterate, the Mongolian, the negro, and the white. At some time every heart experiences the throb of pity; each soul rebels at the indignity of injustice; each vibrates at some moment to the voice of duty, the call of patriotism, or is impelled by the mighty force of love. Not in one age but in every age these feelings have swayed men. The child of kindergarten years and the highly educated, self-disciplined college professor alike feel the elemental emotions. In the one, feeling is manifested in impetuous action. In the other it is restrained, held in check by mature intelligence and cultivated self-control. But in each nature the age-old emotions lie dormant. That is why the little child appeals so often to the mother or some other adult with the words, "Tell me a story." In listening to a story those dormant emotions are awakened and satisfied. That too is why the adult so often becomes absorbed in reading a novel or short story to the degree that he is unconscious of everything around him.

THE USE OF STORIES IN GENERAL EDUCATION

Because the story portrays emotions that are confined to no one region or period of history, and stimulates the emotions of those who hear, it is as potent a means of education to-day as ever it was. Abundant evidence is obtainable of results achieved by story-telling among adults as well as children within the past five or six years. Some of these results have been so remarkable that they seem almost miraculous even to those who obtained them.

Influence of stories during the World War.— Before America became one of the allies in the World War, several drives, undertaken for the purpose of raising funds for the Fatherless Children of France, the Fund for French Wounded, the British War-Orphan Relief, and like relief organizations, did not yield satisfactory returns in some localities. "That is a problem to be solved by the countries involved," was often the reply of those solicited. Consequently, a campaign of story-telling was begun. Skilled narrators studied the field. They made up programs of tales embodying the best traditions of the lands for whose sufferers funds were urgently needed. They chose stories tending to emphasize in a gripping way the reason for the ready response to the call of the colors in the countries where help was needed. They chose also tales picturing the pitiable condition, the seared hopes, and the drab, unbearable future of those who would be beneficiaries of the drive. These stories were told at afternoon teas given under the patronage of society women. They were recounted in schools, in churches, in public libraries, in city parks, wherever and whenever a crowd could be gathered. And whenever they were told, dollars went into the fund, pulled out of the pockets of objectors who had declared the care of far-away folk was not their problem, but who had been made to realize it was the problem of all mankind. In listening to the sad stories, they had seen the plight and the viewpoint of the sufferers. Not only had they seen, but they had vicariously experienced to the point that they had been moved to pity.

Influence of stories in the public school and kindergarten.—A little less than a century ago Froebel made it clear to the world that in hearing stories the emotional life of the child unfolds and develops. As the principles advocated by Froebel were incorporated into the kindergarten, story-telling was given a definite place there. But beyond the kindergarten no provision was made for it in the school curriculum. That it might be of value to older children as well as to those of preschool age, seemingly did not occur to any American educator until about the beginning of the present century. Then it crept into a few private and public experimental schools, and was found to be of great value in illuminating geography and history, in the teaching of civics and nature study, and in leading to an appreciation of literature. Later it was discovered that interest in and enjoyment of both art and music could be enhanced through the medium of the story, and that even technical subjects like arithmetic and spelling could sometimes be enlivened by it. Gradually but steadily the use of stories in the schoolroom increased, until at the present time, in several American cities supervising story-tellers are a part of the elementary school faculty. A number of colleges and universities have added story-telling courses to the curriculum, in order better to equip both grade and high-school teachers for their work. All this has come about because educators have found that systematic, well-planned story-telling is of great value in stimulating the interest of the children in the schoolroom subjects. Lessons learned while interest runs high are impressed deeply and lastingly upon the young mind. Therefore the story, because of its power to lend interest to what otherwise might be dull and unenjoyable, is proving to be a tremendous aid in all schools where it is skillfully and wisely used.

Story-telling in social service work.—In none of the many fields where story-telling is being used is it achieving more gratifying results than in social service work. In public play-grounds, in recreation centers, in settlement houses, in parks and on the streets of the larger towns in the United States story-telling is proving a boon to social-service workers. Through it, as in no other way, has it been possible for the leaders to win the confidence of the so-called "toughs" who gather at all these centers. Through the medium of stories in which rough boys lose themselves, unconsciously higher ethical standards are established, and the seeds of good citizenship are sown.

A boy of the type commonly known as a street bully appeared at a playground in a large Western city not long ago and began abusing the younger children and boasting that he would "clear out the place." As he proceeded to make good his threat the "gypsy story-teller" arrived. (Gypsy story-telling, by the way, is bringing about remarkable results in social-service work. Trained story-tellers in gypsy costume visit playgrounds and other centers. The costume itself is like a lodestone to draw the children. Immediately upon the arrival of the picturesque visitor she is surrounded by a curious group. Seizing her opportunity without delay, she begins a tale through which she presents some lesson the children need to learn.) The boy who intended to "clear out" the playground was as much attracted by the "gypsy" as any of the other children. The first story he heard from her was one of courage, of a lad who substituted for a sick street-sweeper, despite the jeers of his playfellows, in order that the old man might receive pay, even though he could not work. The young bully listened, absorbed from the beginning to the end of the tale. Then he called eagerly, "Tell another one!"

That same boy appeared at the playground regularly for many weeks afterward, but there was no further trouble with him. In the pleasure that came with each visit of the gypsy story-teller and in the appeal of principles her tales emphasized to him, his intention to make trouble melted away.

Dozens of examples can be cited by experienced workers, of the beneficial results of story-telling upon children of the slums.

Story-telling among the adult foreign-born.— Through the medium of the story many Americanization workers are winning the confidence of foreign-born men and women, and are doing more effective work in teaching the meaning of American traditions and awakening loyalty toward the same than they have been able to do in any other way. In New York, Chicago, Boston—almost every great city, in fact, that is coping with the problem of laying the foundation of good citizenship among foreign-born adults as well as children—social-service workers enthusiastically agree that too high a value can hardly be placed upon the story as a tool for the leader and teacher. They bear out their claim by citing examples out of their own experience.

Story-telling in religious instruction.—The story is as valuable a means for the religious teacher as it is for the social-service worker. Children respond naturally to the story. Messages contained in it are received with profound respect and confidence. It influences both habits and thoughts. The story can awaken religious feeling as nothing else can do. It puts listeners into a reverent attitude and makes them fertile soil in which to sow the thought seeds of spirituality. Through the medium of the story the boy or girl can be led to reverence God and his handiwork, to do his or her part toward keeping the laws of Christ vitally operative in society. Patriotic feeling, loyalty to flag and country have been aroused and strengthened down the long span of the ages by the lips of the story-teller. They are being aroused and strengthened now in our great cities by workers who understand that by the wisely chosen narrative the emotions that led to patriotic service are called into play.

The emotions that foster reverence for God also can be awakened through the medium of the story, provided the tale is one that satisfies the intelligence as well as touches the feelings, and, provided the narrator himself takes it seriously.

The Bible the greatest of all story books.— Whoever tells Bible stories skillfully and with sincerity can hardly fail to awaken reverence and establish belief in God, because the Bible is the greatest storybook the world has ever known. Its tales are saturated with human interest. They satisfy both the intellectual and moral sense. The characters are types that appeal to ordinary human beings, because they themselves are so intensely human. One does not need to be refined to the point of fastidiousness in order to understand them. The Old Testament heroes are elemental, faulty men who are rewarded according to their desserts. The men of the New Testament are of much the same type, with the figure of Jesus of Nazareth towering above them like a white flame on a mountain, brightening their lives with his beneficent influence and doctrine, and leading them along paths of righteousness that would not have been chosen but for their belief in him. The Bible stories cover a wide range of interests. They contain spiritual food and pleasure for both the prattling child and the gray-haired grandfather. Tales of little children are in the Book of Israel, and tales of adults that feed little children. There are tales, too, of high endeavor and noble ideals, of picturesque patriarch, impassioned tribal leader, and sumptuous king striving to guide his people along the highway to civic splendor—stories that fire the loftiest emotions of which the adult is capable. Every type of emergency that can arise in life is found somewhere in the Bible, arising in the life of one of its characters. It is an invaluable source of information, entertainment, and comfort for every period of life. It is suited to meet the emotional and spiritual needs of both children and grown-ups.

The combination is ideal—a perfect medium of instruction and material that meets universal needs. Form and content both are suitable. Therefore the degree of success the story-teller in the field of religious education can attain in using this material, depends upon the individual, upon his enthusiasm for the work, upon his skill and industry. In whatever measure he gives to it will results come back to him.

THOUGHT QUESTIONS

1. How were stories used by religious teachers and leaders during antiquity in Greece, China, and other lands?
2. Describe the use of stories by the Hebrews and by Christ; by Buddah, and by Mohammed.
3. What two groups of story-tellers were there in Europe during the Dark Ages? Describe the influence of the missionaries as story-tellers among the tribesmen.
4. What was the first method of systematic education? Describe the first schools of Europe.
5. How was story-telling used in religious and educational work during Mediæval times?
6. How was story-telling used as a method of instruction in Colonial times?

7. What is the secret of the universal appeal of the story? Describe how stories affected standards of life in Norway and various European lands.
8. How is the story being used in educational work to-day, in school and social-service work? In religious work?
9. How does the Bible compare with the other great books of the world as a storybook?

CHAPTER II

THE PURPOSEFUL USE OF THE STORY

SUCCESS with story-telling in the religious field, as in any other, is possible only to the narrator who has a purpose in the use of the story, and who keeps that purpose clearly in mind. He must have a definite idea of what his tales are to accomplish both now and later or he will give them to little purpose. He must understand what transpires in the minds and hearts of his auditors as they follow him, and skillfully lead them along paths where he desires them to go.

AROUSING INTEREST AND SYMPATHY

Interest is the key that unlocks the gate into the realm where educational results are achieved. Being interested in the story, the child follows the characters with eagerness. Interest begets sympathy. Sympathy enables one to share experience with others. In sharing the experiences of the characters, the pupil has a feeling of reality for the truths or principles the story emphasizes. This feeling of reality tends to cause those truths or principles to function in his behavior. Without sympathy on the part of the child toward a story, no benefit will result from his hearing it. Approval, disapproval, pity, disdain, and the various emotions must be awakened. There must be response to all the characters in a narrative as one reacts to the individuals in life. The hearer must feel respect or contempt for them if he is to be swayed by their actions. He must desire to emulate or determine to make himself wholly unlike them. The personages in a tale call forth some real response. They must be noble, base, delightful, or repulsive, as the case may be, to the listener.

Necessity of sustaining interest.—It is clear that the story-teller must aim, first of all, to do that which will arouse interest. But to arouse interest in the beginning is not enough. He must sustain it. From the opening sentence to the closing one his listeners must be keenly alert, for when interest lags, emotions slumber. If there is no eagerness on the part of the children to get each succeeding step in a tale, the narrator talks to little purpose. Therefore whenever he senses an attitude of indifference it behooves him to get at the cause speedily and to remedy it.

This is the most difficult task that confronts the beginner in the field of oral narration, but the right kind of preparation will enable him to begin his tales secure in the knowledge that he will hold attention from the beginning to the end of the story period. If he knows the cause of lagging interest, he can overcome the difficulty, but, like the physician, if the reason for the symptoms is not understood, the prescription may aggravate the ailment instead of acting as a curative.

Reasons for lack of interest.—Indifference on the part of children listening to a story may be due to one or both of two reasons: The tale itself is lacking in dramatic and emotional appeal, which means it is not a suitable one for telling; it is unsuited to the age and understanding of those hearing it; or it is poorly told. Because of unsuitability to the group hearing it, or because of lack of artistry on the part of the narrator, its message is not grasped.

When lack of interest is due to choice of wrong material.—The old adage that an ounce of prevention is worth a pound of cure applies forcefully in the field of story-telling. The trained narrator will never make the mistake of choosing material that is not of the right type for oral presentation, or that is unsuited to the age and development of those hearing it. Even the untrained worker using the graded Sunday-school lessons is not likely to meet with indifference due to the stories themselves, because those included in the leaflets and teachers' guides are supposed to be selected with a view to fitness both as to age suitability and dramatic appeal.

But the mother, the librarian, or settlement worker is likely to be dismayed sometimes to find the audience growing restless when she is reasonably certain she is telling the story well. When this happens, the only thing to do is to get to the end of that tale as soon as possible and begin one that is sure to be liked. Otherwise it will be difficult to hold that same group on future occasions. To the small child—even to those of adolescent years —the story–teller is a magician. For her to give a narrative that fails to delight is to lose her magic in their eyes. She may seem to lose it for a moment, yet become again the enchanter who spirits them into Never-never lands. But to leave with them, when they go from the story period, an impression of having failed, is to make them reluctant to return.

It is imperative that a tale that is received with indifference be succeeded by one that leaves pleasant memories.

When poor presentation is the cause of lack of interest.—Careful preparation will forestall one type of lack of interest. The experienced or trained story-teller never makes the mistake of beginning a tale without knowing that she can tell it well. She understands the disastrous results that are sure to follow slovenly presentation. But the beginner, not realizing that to lose the interest of an individual or a group is to arouse prejudice that will pave her path with difficulty in the future, sometimes plunges into a story without the necessary preparation. When this mistake has been made, and she realizes that the attention of the children is wandering from the thread of the story, she must regain that attention before she ends the tale. Otherwise her audience will go from her believing she does not know how to tell stories, and will not return of their own volition. Children are keen and merciless judges in this matter. Very quickly they sense poor craftsmanship on the part of the narrator. Once she has failed in their eyes they have no regard for her as a story-teller and her power to influence them through stories is at an end.

To regain interest once it has been lost is a very difficult task, but it *can* be done. It can be done by fusing color and action into the various situations, according to methods that, with study and practice, become part of the narrator's equipment. Sometimes it can be done by means of a pause, which serves both to arouse curiosity on the part of the listeners and to provide the story-teller with a moment of thought that makes it possible for her to speed up the action of the tale. These various methods are discussed in detail in the chapter on telling the story.

Providing Useful Knowledge

The arousing of interest and awakening of sympathy are of paramount importance in story-telling, because without them all other aims are impossible. But the narrator who deserves the name is far more than an entertainer. Like the story-teller during the Dark Ages and Mediæval times, he is a teacher, a message-bringer. Always he has some lesson to leave with his listeners; some truth he aims to impress lastingly upon their minds. In order to teach, it is necessary to give useful information. To teach successfully necessitates giving information in such a way that it is received with interest and enthusiasm. Otherwise it is of little lasting benefit, because information received with indifference makes no deep impression. It is not truly learned and therefore does not result either in improved scholarship or desire for better conduct.

The purpose of story-telling in religious education is to build up Christian character, to establish in the child a permanent consciousness of God and a knowledge of the inevitable working of God's laws, developing that consciousness from lower to higher stages; to create an abiding reverential attitude toward all things religious, to establish ideals and strengthen beliefs—all this is involved in the building of Christian character.

Stories that are properly selected contain information concerning the character of God, the Bible, the church, the men and women who have lived noble Christian lives, the hymns, prayers, and other materials used in worship, religious art and artists, and the best thoughts of the great theologians. Stories may be used to teach all of these subjects. It is not necessary that every story told should be the vehicle of new information. But the value of stories for this purpose should have careful consideration.

Giving the child a knowledge of the workings of God's laws.—A factor of tremendous importance in religious education is that of bringing the child, while very young, into a realization of the inevitable workings of God's laws. He needs to learn that the Father he is taught to worship is not only a God of love but a God of justice. There is no escape from paying the penalty that follows violation of his laws. Moral self-control is necessary. For the boy or girl to understand this during the first five or six years of his life is to toughen and strengthen the quality of his moral fiber.

Dr. G. Stanley Hall declares that the slow realization by the child that the laws of God are not evadible and suspendible, but changeless, and that their penalties are as sure as the workings of the laws of nature, is the most important factor of moral and religious training.[1] Therefore this psychologist maintains that in the child's conception of God, he should appear distant and vague, inspiring awe and reverence even more than love; that he should be the God of nature rather than one who administers to the child's individual wants.

[1] *Youth, Its Education, Regimen, and Hygiene*, page 355. D. Appleton & Co., 1922.

For a boy or girl to understand very early that there is no favoritism in God's plan is to render him more amenable to both the moral and the religious code. It makes it possible for him to fit harmoniously into conditions of life that are disagreeable and hard to him, against which, without having gained this knowledge, he might be inclined to rebel.

In other words, the child should be led to see that God's plan embraces the great universe. It is not designed for the comfort or convenience of one individual. No matter how great the desire of that individual may be, it does not bend because of his pleasure. It is a plan of love mighty enough to include all mankind, and to cover not only an hour or a day of life but the entire course. Therefore what ofttimes seems hard about the working of God's laws, is hard only because we do not see our own lives or those of others in an unblurred perspective. We glimpse but the portion that is encompassed within the present. God's plan is devised to work for the welfare of the whole, not just a part. It is because these laws work ultimately for the good of the individual and of the world that they are immutable, like the course of the fixed stars. For the child to realize that he is but an atom in this great plan, instead of the center around which it revolves, is to render him less selfish, and to engender in him consideration for the rights of others, who, like himself, are children of the same heavenly Father, and heirs in the same measure as himself to omnipotent love and care. He who understands that

> "The great God who loveth us,
> He made and loveth all,"

and who believes in the inevitable workings of the laws of that God, is not likely to demand gratification of his own desires and pleasures at the price of discomfort or injury to others.

Bible stories demonstrate the inevitable workings of God's laws.—This realization of the inevitable working of God's laws comes to the boy or girl who hears Bible stories. Throughout the Old Testament —and the New—wrongdoing brings never-failing punishment. When Adam and Eve disobeyed God they were sent out of the Garden Beautiful. When the generations of Noah thought to ignore the Lord and built a tower whose top would reach to heaven, they were scattered abroad upon the face of the earth, unable to understand one another's speech. The wrath of God pursued Jonah when he fled toward Tarshish instead of going to Ninevah. The Bible is so rich in tales that show the inevitable working of God's laws that whoever gives them understandingly and skillfully cannot fail to leave with children the realization that they must obey or pay the penalty. In following the characters in a story this realization comes very vividly.

The value of nature stories.—Tales that illustrate the workings of the laws of nature, which, as demonstrated elsewhere, are religious narratives to the child, help to bring about a realization of the immutability of God's laws. The autumnal season is not prolonged because a husbandman who has devoted his time to pleasure and neglected to gather in his harvest cries vehemently for aid when he sees disaster ahead. Winter comes at the allotted time, and all who have failed to make provision for it must take the consequences. The bees know this, and the squirrels, and all other creatures of the woods and fields, and unfailingly the changing seasons find them prepared. Birds nest and hatch in the spring, because, if they wait until mid-summer, the young will be too weak for the long pilgrimage to warmer regions, or to endure the rigors of winter if they are species that remain through the snow time. If Bible stories and nature tales had no other function in the child's spiritual life, they would be a necessary part of his training, because they make him see that he must obey the laws of God if he would be happy.

INSPIRING CHRISTIAN ATTITUDES

The child may realize the immutability of omnipotent laws, and believe vaguely that God is in all things without growing into a truly Christian character. In order that he may come into a consciousness of God he must *feel* God in the world around him and must have a disposition to obey. He must sense behind the cliffs, groves, and streams hidden, beneficent forces that bespeak good will toward mankind. He must experience a feeling of kinship with nature and with unseen things.

The child is apt to run away from the thought of the disagreeable. Therefore it is of utmost importance that he see obedience as a road to happiness. Goodness for its own sake does not appeal to him, if the way of goodness seems hard. But goodness as a bringer of happiness is very appealing, because happiness is a goal which he can appreciate. Through the medium of the story goodness becomes attractive, the broad highway to the thing that is most desired in life.

The story not merely a source of information.—
In thinking of the story as a medium of religious
education one should not make the mistake of regarding it chiefly as a source of information. Information it does give, and it is necessary that the
child receive much information in order to grow in
Christian character. But giving information is but
a means to an end. As Doctor Betts says, "The
end sought is desired changes in the life, thought,
and experiences of the child." The purpose of the
story is to *mirror life so as to awaken feeling and
desire, to create moods that make possible the estab-
lishment of ideals that shall function in behavior.*

Facts can be taught through abstract axiom
and precept. Through drill and repetition they
can be fixed in the memory as lastingly as the
numerical combinations. But facts hammered into
the mind by a mechanical process do not touch the
heart and quicken the emotions. Therefore such
facts are not likely to create ideals and mould
character.

The great teacners of the world all understood
this, and presented truth through concrete example.
Realizing that they were dealing with vibrant,
throbbing human beings, they used material that
reflected human experience. Living material, skillfully presented, never fails to obtain results. It is
possible to teach many facts that play no part in
shaping ideals. It is possible to give a vast amount
of information the mind will retain, that is not
productive of a single enthusiasm or resolve. But
facts presented through the medium of the story,
truths brought home to the hearer through joy or
distress realized as coming to those who have heeded

or ignored those truths, *do* shape ideals and quicken enthusiasm that affect the daily life.

A girl in an eighth grade in a public school was a source of distress to her teacher and annoyance to the entire class because of her habitual lying. Startling accusations were brought against some of her fellow pupils almost every day. She told wild yarns of experiences to and from school, at home, and on the playground. She charged her parents with acts they never had committed. This practice had been carried on until no one who knew her placed any reliance in what she said. She knew it, yet still she persisted in her falsehoods. She came from a home in which every effort had been made to instil truth in the children. Her wild tales were a source of deep grief to her parents, who had become utterly discouraged in their efforts to make her truthful.

The teacher studied the case from every angle. After conferring with the parents, and learning the methods that had been pursued in the home in attempting to correct the habit, she decided to try the effect of stories. She planned a program of a story each day, one that was full of action and interest to the pupils and in which the effect of lying, misrepresentation, or exaggeration was emphasized. It required much tact, and much hard work to make out such a program, for that teacher knew well that tales crudely pointing a moral would antagonize the girl. By going to many sources for material, however, she finally obtained enough stories of the type she needed to fill the recreation story period for a month.

The girl in question was an eager listener whenever tales were told. She was particularly fond of stories, and expressed a marked liking for several that made up the various programs. On two occasions, when pupils were to write a composition on some subject of their own choosing, she wrote reviews of the tales that had especially appealed to her. But no change was observed in her conduct. She told falsehoods as freely at the end of the third week of story programs as she had told them at the beginning. The teacher felt decidedly discouraged, yet she determined not to give up in her effort to effect some improvement in the habits of a pupil who was in all other respects most likable.

Toward the end of the fourth week she told a story of a soldier in the Russian army who was executed because of the misrepresentation of one of his comrades. The youth had not maliciously set out to destroy the boy, but in the hope of gain to himself had circulated a report he meant later on to acknowledge as false. The accuser was sent with a message from his commander to a general in a distant province, and upon his return was horrified to find that during his absence his comrade had faced a firing squad.

Unmistakably the girl was deeply affected by the tale. Throughout the remainder of the afternoon she seemed depressed and restless. The following morning she came to school early. Meeting the teacher as she approached the building, she asked if she might go in and help her. Upon getting into the room she burst into tears. "Miss Adams," she exclaimed, "I've made you a lot of trouble by telling things that were not true, but I'm never going to do it again. That story you told yesterday makes me shiver whenever I think of it. I never dreamed that making up things when you don't mean to do any harm could cause anything as terrible as that."

As nearly as was possible, considering the force of long habit, the girl kept to her resolve. The improvement in her became very marked, and from a pupil so untruthful that she was nicknamed by her classmates "Lying Patsy," she grew to be one whose word could be thoroughly relied upon.

The transformation effected by the story in this case is not unusual in the experience of narrators. Habits of falsehood, cruelty, slovenliness, laziness, and rudeness have been overcome, sometimes by a single tale, often by the systematic and regular telling of stories tending to correct those tendencies. There is no trait that needs to be cultivated in a child, no mood or desire that needs to be created, that cannot, generally speaking, be cultivated or created through the telling of the apt story. In the same way, through the medium of the story, undesirable traits can be overcome.

There are, it is true, children who are seemingly in conflict with any system of instruction, no matter how delightful that system may be to the average, normal child, and occasionally the most skillful story-tellers using ideal material fail to obtain the results they have hoped to obtain. But the child who does not yield to the appeal of the story is not a normal child. Moreover, he is very rare. The average child responds as unfailingly to tales as he responds to the urge to play. His ethical life can be enriched and beautified by them. By them his religious life can be nurtured into full flower.

The attitudes of the young child similar to those of primitive man.—The very young child resembles primitive man in the time when he worshiped the sun and endowed animals with supernatural qualities. Out of this sun adoration and animistic belief grew the world's first stories, the nature myths and fairy tales that have become our nursery narratives. They were religious stories to the jungle and hill men who first told them. They are saturated with primeval belief in the power of the sun and other saving forces of nature that in them figure as the wise and beneficent fairy godmother, a king devoted to the welfare of his subjects, or some other protecting creature.

Ancient stories early man's explanation of the mysteries of nature.—These ancient stories are redolent of awe and longing, of desire to know about the vast unknown beyond the narrow confines of the tribal camp ground. The groping, eager tellers peopled this world of mystery with characters such as they desired and hoped its inhabitants to be. These primitive narratives were to early man what science is to the people of to-day, an explanation of forces that perpetually aroused their wonder, an account of the origin of the oceans, peaks, and rivers that hemmed them in. Having no way of getting at the truth, their imaginings concerning all that was mystery ran wild. In talking to each other they portrayed causes as they fancied them to be.

That this was the case even during the Middle Ages we know from legends of the twelfth and thirteenth centuries that have come down to us. Crusaders returning from Palestine came by the Liparian Islands, where, on Vulcano and Stromboli are numerous openings due to volcanic agencies that geologists know as fumeroles. From time to time these holes emit smoke and sulphurous vapors, some of them intermittently, some almost without cessation. This manifestation of heat forces within the earth has been going on there for centuries, and when the crusaders came within sight and smell of a phenomenon that is now well understood, they fled from the vicinity in terror.

Shortly afterward, throughout Italy, Germany, France, and England there spread a story that on this island group below the boot of Italy was an open passage into hell. Men who had traveled that way had seen proof of it in the smoke and fumes that poured out of a great black hole. This story thus circulated became a powerful factor in developing certain moral attitudes.

Another belief current throughout France and Switzerland during the Middle Ages, and held there even yet by the peasantry in some districts, is that the great bowlders so common in this region were brought from the Alps by a race of giants. Geologists know they were carried down by vanished glaciers, but only within the last century, when Louis Agassiz spent an entire summer on the Lauteraar glacier and made an exhaustive study of the work of the moving ice, did they find out the truth. But the belief handed down from ancient times had become so deep-rooted that it is not yet eradicated. There is a lengthy cycle of fairy stories told by French and Swiss peasants that center around these bowlders.

The American Indians in the Lake Willoughby region of Vermont had a legend that the rocks along the shore and within the bed of that body of water—also deposited by glaciers—were once a race of warriors turned to stone by the Great Spirit *because of their ceaseless fighting*. The tribes of northern California believed Mount Shasta was the tepee of the Great Spirit, and the smoke that sometimes poured out of an opening near the summit —evidence of the volcanic nature of the mountain —came from a fire the Mighty One kept eternally burning within it to keep him warm.

Similar legends cluster around the volcanoes of the South Seas. The Indians of the Grand Canyon region have a wonder story of how that gorge came to be. And so we find it in the tales of all primitive peoples. Through them move wicked giants who are conquered or destroyed by greater and better forces, *a reflection of desire on the part of bewildered tribesmen for right to triumph over wrong, for warmth and light ever to be victorious over the monsters of darkness*. The repetition and reiteration of tales in which these destructive forces were overcome gave early man a sense of protection, of security in a world awesome and mysterious.

The little child repeats many of the experiences of his aboriginal forefathers. The mystery and vastness of the world about him arouses wonder, longing, awe. One has but to observe his reaction to a gorgeous sunset, a hillside swathed in flowers, or the rhythmic boom of the ocean as breakers whip the shore to realize the truth of this statement. Both the questions he asks and the expression of face and eyes as he gazes on the marvel, reflect his wonder and desire to know the cause. Very often, in that expression, as well as in his queries, wonderment and awe are mingled. *It is the business of the religious teacher to see to it that he feels this force to be friendly toward him and senses God in it, instead of regarding it as somethimg to be feared.*

Attitude of young child toward nature essentially religious.—The problem of inspiring the child with a God-consciousness during his early years is greatly simplified, because his attitude toward nature is essentially religious. His heart and mind are like a fertile field, plowed, harrowed and ready for the seed of the sower. The seed will germinate as does that scattered in rich loam soil when every condition is propitious. It is of utmost importance that this seed be planted now. A consciousness of God needs to be awakened in the child while he is reaching out to receive it. At no other time in his life is he so responsive to unknown forces around him. No impressions are as lasting as his earliest ones. The influences of the first five or six years of his life are more potent in shaping his ideals and attitudes than are any others. He who has seen and felt God in nature during early childhood is not likely, when an adult, to lose that God-consciousness. Men who have traveled the highway of crime have been regenerated through some happening that aroused in them a dormant God-consciousness and bearing toward righteousness established in childhood.

The story the most powerful means of inspiring God-consciousness.—No means available to the religious leader is as effective as the story in inspiring this God-consciousness, and in nurturing it once it has been inspired. Because of its power to make situations real and vivid, the story has potentialities for touching the sensitive chords of feeling, and to render more responsive and vibrant those already awakened. The account of the creation, simply and dramatically told, with emphasis on God's wisdom in putting man into the world, and protecting him after placing him there, like a loving, thoughtful father, arouses reverence and a sense of security in a world vast and often terrifying. To hear that the mountains and rivers are his handiwork, "the seas and all that in them is," and that the same wisdom and tenderness have gone into the fashioning of a beetle as in the creating of man, the lord of the universe, will give a child a sense of kinship with nature and a regard for all of God's creatures that will not depart from him. Years of neglect in his later training may submerge this early impression, or blur it, but it will not be wholly effaced. The right influence will rekindle the old reverence.

God-consciousness must be developed from lower stages to higher.—Besides inspiring the child with a consciousness of God, and leading him to see the inevitable working of God's laws, it is the mission of the religious teacher to develop this consciousness from lower to higher stages. This means that once reverence for God and belief in him are established, they must be fed and nurtured. The husbandman who deserves the name does not sow a field and then leave it neglected for tares to creep in and dwarf the tender growths. The human plant requires as much care as corn or wheat. From the beginning on through the days of adolescence the work of nurturing should be continued in order to meet the needs of boys and girls in the various stages of development. All along the way they should be led to see the hand of God in the world; to know that as he was with the people of Israel, strengthening them according to their needs and rewarding them according to their merits, so is he with his people to-day. By concrete example, by portraying men living their lives and working out their destinies, the story makes this clear.

The Bible holds sufficient story material to feed the boy or girl from early childhood to maturity, and *to continue feeding him after adult years are reached*. P. W. Wilson,[1] writing recently, speaks in these words, of the Bible as the great book for all the ages of man: "The Bible is not only a shrine in itself; it is a portal. Unless you know your Bible, Rubens and Rembrandt, Durer and Giotto, yes, and Sargent when he painted prophets for Boston instead of portraits for Britain, leave you far behind. For anything except the good it spoils the palate. It is a genuine preservative of what ought to endure. It was in the Bible that John Bunyan found the cadences of his *Pilgrim's Progress*, John Bright the majestic simplicity of his speeches, and Abraham Lincoln his Gettysburg address. It is to be doubted whether any statesman or any writer has risen to real eminence without having the Bible in him."

One of the salient characteristics of those in adolescent years is an eagerness for immediate results, a desire for sowing without reaping. Precept and admonition are usually futile in making them see that there can be no lasting structure without a carefully laid foundation. But the story,

[1] *Literary Review*, January 12, 1924.

with its picturing of life, *can* make them see it. Therefore the well-chosen and skillfully told narrative has a salutary effect during this "age of intemperate haste," as the adolescent period has been called, that cannot be overestimated.

Summary of chapter.—Summing up, then, the purpose of the story in religious education is to build Christian character. In order to do this it is necessary to awaken religious feeling in the child, reverence for God and his handiwork, and to inspire him with a God-consciousness that will result in creating standards and establishing ideals. It is necessary also to bring to him a realization of the inevitable working of God's laws, yet at the same time to feel good will in the working of those laws, and sufficient dependence on that good will to render him obedient, no matter at what cost, to ideals that he feels represent the noblest and best in life.

This aim can be achieved only by arousing interest in and appreciation of suitable subject matter, subject matter that mirrors life in such a way that the child sees and feels that which it is necessary for him to see and feel, and, through seeing and feeling, comes into *understanding* and *reverence*.

Therefore the preparation of the story-teller must be twofold: 1. He must equip himself to tell stories so skillfully and sympathetically that he cannot fail to arouse both interest and sympathy. 2. He must be able to choose material that tends to inspire God-consciousness, and that will bring to his hearers the knowledge of the inevitable workings of God's laws it is imperative that they should have.

THOUGHT QUESTIONS

1. What are the reasons for lack of interest on the part of those hearing a story?
2. What is the necessary procedure on the part of the story-teller when a story fails to interest because of being unsuited to those hearing it?
3. How is it possible to regain interest?
4. What is the purpose of story-telling in religious education?
5. What knowledge should be given a child in order for him to realize the purpose of story-telling in religious education?
6. Explain the value of Bible stories in showing the working of God's laws; of nature stories.
7. Why is it important that the little child see obedience as a road to happiness?
8. How is it possible, through the use of stories, to inspire a child with a consciousness of God?

CHAPTER III

THE STRUCTURE OF THE STORY

A FRENCH psychologist once made the statement that there are as many different stories in the world as pebbles. When one thinks of the countless narratives that printed pages hold, and then remembers the vast number of others that comprise the spoken literature of various countries, narratives that never have been put into book form, but that have been handed down generation after generation by word of mouth, and are still repeated at peasant firesides, in huts and tepees, where the ways of life are primitive, one realizes that the statement is no exaggeration.

The South Sea islander has his myths and legends that, night after night, are recounted under the moon and stars. The Ethiopian in the African jungles, the mountaineers of Afghanistan, the plainsmen of Farther India, the shepherds of the Balkans, the Eskimo in the frozen northlands, and the Indians of the Americas all have hundreds of stories, tales that have passed from the old to the young and from century to century by the tongues of men and women. These all make up a literature as carefully preserved and definitely established as an expression of a people's thought as is much of the French or the English literature. Besides these tales there are millions upon millions of narratives in books, so many that an attempt to estimate the number bewilders one. Truly the stories in the world seem as innumerable as pebbles.

ALL GREAT STORIES ARE ALIKE IN STRUCTURE

Each tale that deserves the name is distinct and different from every other tale, yet in one respect they are all alike. They are the same in structure. The nature myth of the Fiji tribesman and the highly artistic narrative of Hugo, Dickens, or Turgenieff are built according to the same pattern. The framework around which their creators have woven them is the same in every land. The skeleton used by Joseph Conrad or Blasco Ibáñez to-day was used also by the aboriginal men who, out of their fear and wonder concerning nature, fashioned the first tales the world knows. The only difference is, early man did not analyze as he built, and consciously follow any formula or set of rules. The present-day narrator, whether his yarns be spoken or written, has evolved, through a study of old stories and the elements in them that awakened and held the interest of men, a technique and knowledge of structure that he follows as punctiliously as the painter follows his formula for obtaining color combinations. Wherever he follows this formula, provided he has also intelligence and enthusiasm for story-telling, he does not fail of success.

All primitive tales dramatic because of conflict.— All primitive peoples had a highly developed sense of the dramatic, due to the fact that the environment in which they lived teemed with mystery. Life was a tense and highly exciting drama to them.

Eagerness to know about the forces of nature, which they did not understand, kept suspense constantly keyed to a high pitch. Always they were wondering about what was going to happen to them. When a tempest raged, an avalanche roared, or lightning streaked the sky, terror was mingled with wonder. It is because these stories reflect Nature, the Mysterious, and portray the lives of those who lived in fear of nature, that they abound in suspense and surprises.

The narrator on the Asiatic highlands before the Aryans set forth on the great migration, gave to his fellows tales replete with the suspense the world held for him. With the opening sentences he pictured to them in a terse, spectacular way the setting of his narrative, and introduced the character or characters moving through it. He kept these characters in constant action from start to finish, and let down the curtain upon the last scene in the moment when the curiosity of his auditors was satisfied as to the outcome, but while interest and sympathy were still running high. He gave to them what satisfied himself as an explanation of something that had aroused his curiosity or kindled his fear. The only satisfactory explanation involved characters in conflict, as the forces of nature seemed to be, darkness and light ever struggling to overcome each other,—wind and calm, heat and cold. He too was in a constant struggle for existence with wild animals that prowled upon his camp place. Life to him was an endless battle to keep from becoming food for some other creature, and to obtain enough food for himself to ward off starvation. Always he carried with him some unsatisfied desire. Therefore he introduced conflict and desire into his stories. They made up the essence of his life.

STORIES ABOUND IN DRAMATIC INTEREST

The element of conflict and desire that entered so largely into the racial tales is what scholars to-day know as *dramatic interest*. It is conflict between human beings, between human beings and animals, between human beings and the forces of nature, or between animals and some opposing force. Animal stories hold suspense because they deal with living creatures, but tales of flowers, trees, and mountains do not, unless they are personified. Suspense is aroused only where conscious life is involved.

The conflicting forces of nature were a source of suspense to early man, not because of themselves, but because he imagined them to be living, purposeful creatures, and because of the possible outcome of their struggle to each other and to himself. A story is dramatic only when it keeps the listener or reader in suspense as to the outcome and its effect upon the character or characters. It can arouse suspense only when there is conflict between the characters themselves, or between the characters and an opposing force or forces. The characters *must be conscious, living, purposeful creatures.*

Conflict between the forces of nature that does not in any way affect life may be mighty, but it is not dramatic. Suspense comes only with knowledge of living creatures in difficulty or danger. An avalanche in an uninhabited part of the mountains or volcanic eruption on some unpeopled desert isle is in itself interesting to the scientist, but they do not stir the world at large because they do not affect life.

A storm at sea may be terrible and spectacular as beheld from a distance, yet arouse no emotion in those who view it save admiration and awe of nature's power. But if a ship is tossing at the mercy of that tempest, with every moment likelihood of being destroyed, that same gale becomes intensely dramatic. Suspense runs high in all who see, hear, and know of the plight of the vessel. Fear, hope, anguish, and kindred emotions are aroused because of the possible fate of crew and passengers.

A story to be dramatic must deal with active, intelligent creatures.—Many attempts have been made by those interested in nature study to give children stories about inanimate objects alone— trees, flowers, stones, stars, and mountains. Where these objects have been personified and endowed with the attributes of human beings the writers have succeeded. But they have succeeded only because of having introduced *human elements* into their tales. Yet even the best of such stories are not highly popular with boys and girls. Artificiality is detected in them. Being written by those who did not *believe* the objects to be human, children sense a false note. Yet the primitive nature myths and animal tales, and the narratives that have grown out of the earliest forms of religion, do interest those who hear them, because they have come from those who believed the forces of nature to be monstrous, living, purposeful, struggling things.

Very few modern writers have succeeded in personifying the moon and stars with sufficient conviction that their tales have gripped the young folk to whom they were told. But the Greek stories of Apollo, Phæton, Orion, or the Pleiades are received with enthusiasm if recounted to those in the age period for which they have an appeal. These ancient myths were believed by the people who gave them to the world. The glowing heavenly bodies were striving, living creatures to them, and even very young children sense the difference between the ancient narratives that are true in spirit and "nature-fakir" tales of later origin. The former were true to those who first told them. They ring with sincerity even to-day. Consequently, they have lived and influenced throughout the ages. The modern narrative in which nature is personified has seldom endured for a decade.

All the great modern stories abound in conflict.— The racial tales abound in conflict. Early man was filled with wonder concerning the effect upon his own life or that of some of his fellows, of a force he feared or against which he struggled. The great modern narratives abound in conflict because conflict is still the essence of life. The days of man even now are made up of struggle for success and happiness, of perpetual effort to realize deep desires. The authors of these stories understood that tales that deserve the name must reflect real life. Whatever portrays life truthfully must be a fabric of conflict and desire.

Primitive man did not dissect and analyze. His tales are rich in dramatic interest because they are slices out of life, which to him was an unending span of suspense. He introduced conflict into them, not for effect, but spontaneously. Just as he called for help to the sun or for deliverance from the ravages of a flood or tempest, so he put struggle, the only thing he knew, into his tales.

It is because of the spontaneity of these racial tales that they have lived on through the centuries. The work of man who writes for effect or for material gain seldom outlasts a few seasons. Present-day authors whose creations really grip are those who are portraying life truthfully and with sincerity rather than with merely studied artistry; who write because they have a message that cannot be withheld. And the age-old appeal of truth and sincerity brings to their work a success and longevity that often far exceeds their expectations. Their tales are replete with the conflict that engenders suspense. They are full of human interest. Blasco Ibáñez, the famous Spanish novelist, already referred to, said in a recent interview: "Literature to-day is as it was in the days of the ancients. The same elements comprise it. The same formulas hold. The only difference is that it reflects different conditions, a different philosophy and point of view."

Dramatic situations not necessarily those of physical activity.—Tales that abound in conflict are not necessarily those of physical achievement. The account of the struggle of a man with himself in an effort to overcome a vice or moral failing may be as replete with interest to those who read and hear as that of him who conquers by muscular strength. One of the most moving narratives in the Bible is that of Christ's agony in the garden, as related in the twenty-second chapter of Luke. No physical activity marks the struggle. Among the great secular tales of the world are many of this same type, in which a spiritual struggle, rather than a physical one, is involved. But, in the main, such narratives as these are not of interest to boys and girls below the age of twelve or fourteen. There are some tales in which the conflict is solely of the spirit and to which small children respond whole-heartedly, but that is because, like primitive man, the little child is apt to think of hatred, deceit, and the various vices as monsters. But to the boy or girl who wants to hear about heroes who *do things,* the story of men struggling with themselves is not interesting. The lad of ten or twelve does not think of vices as living creatures. He wants physical activity. It is the older, adolescent youth who is gripped by accounts of a fight to be victorious over haterd or selfishness.

The Parts of the Story

Beginning the story.—Every properly constructed story is composed of four distinct parts: (1) the beginning, (2) the body, (3) the climax, and (4) the conclusion. The beginning of a story, to those who hear it, is like the first impression of a person upon the strangers he meets. If the initial meeting leaves the feeling that he is a likable and well-meaning individual, there is a desire to see more of him. If, on the contrary, he seems colorless or disagreeable the average man or woman will not strive to know him better.

It is the same with a story. If interest is aroused by the opening sentences, those who hear will listen eagerly in order to find out what comes next.

Conflict must appear in the beginning.—In every well-constructed story, especially if it is a story to be told, conflict appears at the very beginning, sometimes in the first sentence, always in the first two or three paragraphs. This means that the characters are introduced the minute the curtain is drawn back revealing the scene. The aborigine in the uplands of Asia did this. So does the skillful writer of the twentieth century, and so has every successful creator of stories down the ages.

Usually, in the first two or three paragraphs the atmosphere of the tale is created. The setting of the story is made clear. But this must be done deftly and skillfully. Beyond a sentence or two there must not be a description of time or place in which no characters are present.

Some novelists, like Scott, have devoted pages to a description of time and place before the characters get into action. But when that which is nonessential to the unraveling of the plot has been cut away, even in Scott we find beginnings as they were in the ancient nature myth. The characters come upon the stage and get into action at once, and they continue to be in action until the curtain goes down on the scene.

The beginning paragraph of a story that is told may also give the concept of the tale. It may make clear to the hearer what issues are involved. But if the concept is given in the beginning, it must be given with skill. It should be a part of the characterization, not an abstract statement. Interest is not keenly aroused when one hears, "The story I am going to tell you is about a boy who lost faith in his best friend just because he did not understand something that happened." But interest is instantly focused on the words of the narrator who says, "Until the day of the Carlton-Scoville meet, Frank Norton believed Ned Peters was the most loyal friend a boy could have. Then Ned fell down so completely in his eyes that, as the fellows got into their track suits, he felt very sure he never could trust him again."

Concept, like atmosphere and time, must be introduced along with the characters if interest is to be aroused in the beginning of the story. The hearer must immediately see characters in action, or he will not be keenly alert as to what is about to happen.

Necessity of getting characters into action.—The necessity of getting the characters into action the minute the story opens cannot be emphasized too strongly. The printed narrative, the messages of which are carried to the mind through the medium of the eye, may have one page, even several paragraphs or pages, devoted to a description of characters or locality, and yet be interesting and delightful to the reader. There are many great stories the charm and strength of which lie almost entirely in character drawing and portrayal of setting. They are tales in which suspense is aroused by the conflicting characteristics of the person who moves, or persons who move, through them. But they are not narratives to be told. The spoken tale must abound in action, and that action must begin with the beginning of the story.

The beginning in racial tales.—The beginning of an ancient folk-tale from Picardy illustrates what is meant by saying conflict must be introduced with the opening of the story.

"A very long time ago Crepin and the devil combined their savings and bought a large piece of land. The devil, for his part of the proceeds the first year, demanded everything that came from the soil. Crepin might have everything beside that.

"Crepin pretended to be satisfied with this one-sided bargain, but made up his mind to play a trick on the devil."

Likewise in the following old narrative of Lorraine:

"A king had three sons, and, becoming old, he wished to give his sovereign power to one of them and live his declining years in peace. So he called them to him and said: 'I am broken with age and can no longer be burdened with affairs of state. But I love the three of you equally, and cannot choose one above the others to wear the crown. So I shall impose a task upon each of you. Whichever succeeds first in bringing to me the largest and smallest needles in the world shall become lord of my palace and kingdom.'"

An old version of the legend of the Flying Dutchman begins like this:

"Once upon a time a Dutch ship set sail from the East Indies to return to Holland. The Dutch had rich lands in the East Indies and many a poor lad went out from his home before the mast and landed in Java, where he settled himself and grew rich.

"Such an one was a certain Deidrich, who had no father or mother living, and was left to shift for himself. When he came to Java he was bound out to a rich planter; but he worked so hard and so faithfully that it was not long before he was free and his own master. Little by little he saved his money, and as he was very careful, it was not many years before he was very rich indeed."

The openings of these stories are similar to those of thousands of racial tales that have come down from the remote days of antiquity, every one of which, from the standpoint of structure, is a perfect narrative for telling. There is no detailed description in them. In each one action begins in the first paragraph, or there is a suggestion of the conflict that marks that tale. An idea is given of the thing that is to be overcome, and consequently interest is aroused at once.

The beginnings of the notable modern stories are in structure like those of the old tales. In *The Pony Engine and the Pacific Express* William Dean Howells gives an idea of time, characters, and concept: "Christmas Eve, after the children had hung up their stockings and got all ready for St. Nic, they climbed up on papa's neck to kiss him good night, and when they both got their arms around his neck, they said they were not going to bed till he told them a Christmas."

Louise E. Chollet begins the ever-popular story of *Blunder* thus:

"Blunder was going to the Wishing-Gate to wish for a pair of Shetland Ponies and a little coach like Tom Thumb's."

In Arthur Ransome's delightful book entitled *Old Peter's Russian Tales*, an idea of setting and hero is given in the opening paragraph:

"Somewhere in the forest of great trees—a forest so big that the forests of England are little woods beside it—is the hut where old Peter lives."

On through a wide range of both ancient and

modern tales we might go and find in all of them these same characteristics: *Action begins with the opening paragraph, or characters are introduced in such a way as to suggest the action that is to follow. Time, place, atmosphere, and concept are introduced along with the characters.*

Bible tales examples of perfect beginnings.— The Bible stories are examples of tales with perfect beginnings, because in them interest is aroused by the first sentences.

In the opening chapter of Genesis the character is God, and in the first sentence action begins— something is done:

"In the beginning God created the heaven and the earth. And the earth was without form and void, and darkness was upon the face of the deep." There was something to overcome, something to improve and make better.

In the call of Abram, in the twelfth chapter of Genesis, we find: "Now the Lord had said unto Abram, Get thee out of thy country and from thy father's house, unto a land which I will show thee."

What do we find? A picture of a man about to depart from a land dear to him. Something is about to happen. The child knows it as he hears that opening sentence, and is eager for the unfolding of the plot. He wants to see whether or not Abram obeys, and what comes of his action.

Through countless chapters of the Old Testament we might go and find always beginnings that introduce characters and awaken interest with their suggestion of something about to happen. It is the same with the New Testament. Nowhere in literature do we find such flawless stories from the standpoint of structure as those of the Gospels, the Epistles, and the Acts of the Apostles:

"Now when Jesus was born in Bethlehem of Judæa in the days of Herod the King, there came wise men from the east to Jerusalem."

"Seeing the multitude, he went up into a mountain, and when he was set his disciples came unto him."

"And it came to pass in those days that there went out a decree from Cæsar Augustus that all the world should be taxed.

"And all went to be taxed, every one to his own city.

"And Joseph also went up from Galilee, out of the city of Nazareth, into Judæa, unto the city of David, which is called Bethlehem."

Upon hearing these beginnings interest is aroused as to what will happen next, and the reader or hearer is not disappointed. Something does happen, right through the body of the story, until suspense reaches its apex in the climax. Action is sustained from the opening to the close of the tale. When the action is completed the story ends dramatically and satisfactorily to the hearer, without an unnecessary word.

The dramatic splendor of the Bible stories is what makes them so appealing to boys and girls. The recital of happenings of the long ago in the unaffected, forceful style of the Hebrew narrators gives them an interest that holds as keenly now as when they were first heard by the primitive Oriental folk, a people who were men in stature but children in thought, as are all primitive peoples. They mean as much to children to-day as they meant to the grown-up children of Israel. Something of the child nature survives in every human being, no matter how old. Therefore these ancient narratives rich in suspense never become antiquated. To adults as well as to children they are and always will be incomparably interesting. Even if they had no religious value they would stand alone as flawlessly constructed tales.

There is no unvarying rule or formula for beginning the oral story other than the one already given. The beginning may be narrative or dialogue in style. Each has been and can be used with success. But the novice in the field of story-telling will find narrative easier to handle. Dialogue, as one ushers in the characters, is somewhat difficult. After being fairly well launched, the tale may abound in conversation, but for the first two or three paragraphs, unless one is very expert, it is well to keep away from it.

The body, climax, and conclusion of the story.— From the beginning the action continues on through what is known as the body of the story. Here one incident follows another in rapid succession. One act or happening contributes to or causes that which succeeds it. For this reason the interest of those who hear or read is constantly increasing. Steadily and rapidly suspense grows. There is eagerness to know the outcome or fate of the characters, until that eagerness reaches its apex or highest pitch in the point we know as the climax. Then the mystery is explained or the solution given, and directly the curtain goes down on the scene.

The climax of the story, like the beginning and body, must contain no extraneous matter. In the climax the great point of the narrative is revealed. Interest reaches its pinnacle as this point is revealed. As soon as the point is made clear, interest begins to decline.

After the climax has been reached, the end follows speedily in the conclusion. The conclusion also must contain nothing that is not necessary. It must not detract from or spoil what has gone before. Never must it moralize or put into words what the narrator *thinks* about any of the characters or their actions. To do that is to create an anticlimax. The conclusion *pleasingly finishes* the story, leaving what has preceded to work out its own interpretation and moral in the minds of those who have heard. The conclusion ushers the characters off the stage in a way that satisfies the mind.

The following examples show the perfection of the body, climax, and conclusion structure of Bible stories:

In the first chapter of Genesis, light envelops the universe, "a firmament in the midst of the water" is created, the seas are divided from the land; grass, herbs, and trees appear. The sun, moon, and stars are set in the sky, and creatures of land and water are made. Then comes the climax, the place where interest runs highest. Man is created in the image of God and given dominion over the beasts.

Then, simply and dramatically, without in any way depreciating what has gone before, the story is finished in a satisfactory manner.

"And God saw everything that he had made, and behold, it was very good. And the evening and the morning were the sixth day.

"And on the seventh day God ended his work

which he had made; and he rested on the seventh day from all the work which he had made.

"And God blessed the seventh day and sanctified it; because that in it he had rested from his work which God created and made."

There is no limit to the number of scenes or pictures that comprise a story, so long as each is necessary to the unfolding of the plot. Some tales consist of less than half a dozen situations, while some have fifteen, twenty, and even more. But *each must contribute something to the one that succeeds it*. Otherwise it has no purpose in the story and should be cut away.

Study of many stories necessary.—The student who aspires to become a successful story-teller should study many narratives with a view to carefully observing beginnings, body, climax, and ending, using for this purpose both Bible and secular tales. In the secular field he will do well to confine his observation largely to fairy tales, myths, and legends that have come down the ages, the racial stories that grew out of the religion and life of primitive man, and that, like the Bible tales, are untouched by artificiality. It will be well also to read analytically some of the works of the great modern masters, Hugo, Maupassant, Daudet, Turgenieff, René Bazin, Poe, Nathaniel Hawthorne and men of equal standing in the world of literature, to see how unvaryingly they have kept to the principles embodied in the racial tales. There are many excellent contemporary stories, but if the student scans the best of those mentioned above he will very likely have as much work on this one theme as time will allow. Since there cannot be a study of all well-constructed narratives, it is advisable to give one's attention to those that have stood the test of time.

Summary.—A story, considered from the standpoint of structure, consists of four parts. The beginning must never be a rambling introduction. Characters must be ushered in with the opening sentences and action start at once; there must be a suggestion that something is going to happen.

Once the action starts it must move swiftly and without a break through the body of the tale toward the climax, with all the time suspense being maintained, until it reaches its highest point in the climax.

The climax reached, the story should be brought to a close without delay, but not abruptly. There should be just enough words to get the characters off the stage in a manner that seems logical and otherwise satisfying to the hearer.

THOUGHT QUESTIONS

1. In what respect are all great stories alike?
2. What is meant by dramatic interest in a story?
3. Are dramatic situations necessarily those of physical activity?
4. Where must conflict enter into a story?
5. What should the opening paragraphs of a story contain? Mention a Bible story that is an illustration of a model beginning.
6. What is meant by the body of a story? What is meant by unnecessary incidents in a story? Why do unnecessary incidents spoil a good story?
7. Of what does the climax of a story consist? The conclusion? Give examples of model climaxes and conclusions in Bible stories.

CHAPTER IV

THE STORY INTERESTS OF CHILDREN

IF story-telling is to be a power in building Christian character, the material used must be suited to the age and understanding of those to whom it is given. A perfectly constructed tale may be exquisitely told, yet make no appeal to those who hear it because it is too old or too young for them. The boy in the late period of adolescence will not thrill at a recital of happenings among brownies and gnomes, nor will the lad who craves tales of physical adventure be entertained by an account of a man's heroic struggle to overcome a weakness or defect of character. The one has grown beyond interest in brownies and gnomes. The other has not yet come into a comprehension of the mighty drama of an individual in conflict with his own spirit. Each individual responds only to those stories that reflect his world or his desires, or that reflect an environment different from his own, about which he feels curiosity.

THE INTERESTS OF YOUNG CHILDREN

The world of the small child lies within narrow boundaries. It is made up of persons and objects he can see, hear, and touch, that are or have been part of his experience. The account of a potentate in the Congo who wears rings in his ears and nose and bedecks himself with feathers will not satisfy his longings, because African chiefs are outside the range of his experience. His imagination is not yet unfolded to the point that it carries him among personalities and conditions that are grotesque and strange. He is a realist, this small person of from three to six, and is concerned only with his immediate world. Members of his family, relatives, neighbors, other children, pets—creatures he can see and hear, or that he has seen and heard— all interest him, because they are part of his environment.

Stories for little children must deal with the familiar.—The mother who takes care of him whether he is sick or well, and the father who brings home money that buys his food and provides for his material wants, fill a large part of his world. Almost to a like degree the fathers and mothers of other little boys and girls interest him, because they are like his own parents. He is concerned about his sisters and brothers for the same reason that he is concerned about his father and mother. They are part of his life. They are like him in many ways. His interest runs high regarding other children because he looks upon them as kindred beings. He wonders about the things they do— how fast they can run, what skill they have in manipulating toys, and what they like to eat. He asks countless questions about them, questions that have grown out of his own difficulties, desires, and experiences. He wonders if other small people have interests, annoyances and satisfactions as he has. Any one who observes little children will find them asking such questions as these of other children: "What is your name? Where do you live? What do you like to play? Have you a dog or a kitty? Can you run fast?"

Countless other interrogations are plied whenever tiny tots meet. Each one grows out of a desire or an experience.

A tale may be ideal for little children in general, perfect in age suitability, and a prime favorite in half a dozen lands, yet make no appeal to certain individual children or groups of children, because it abounds in characters and incidents remote from their experience. The child of the city slums, who never has seen barnyard animals, green fields, and running brooks, will not delight in a tale of country life, unless through creatures already known, or through some familiar medium he can see pictures of horses, cows, and sheep, streams and fields. Likewise, little people in a sequestered village will have no satisfaction in a tale portraying the experiences of children in a subway, or among the skyscrapers of Manhattan. They will enjoy such stories if through making a comparison between the railroads and trains they know, or the houses with which they are familiar, the narrator enables them to visualize subways and forty-story buildings. In the same way, contrasting dogs and cats with horses, cows, and sheep, or the plant in the school-room window with trees of the forest, will enable the city child who never has been beyond his crowded tenement quarter to understand and respond to a story of country life. The gap between the familiar and the unfamiliar must be bridged before pleasure or benefit can come to a child through a story.

Conversation of children evidences their story interests.—The surest way in which the narrator can obtain a knowledge of the story interests of early childhood is to listen to the conversation of little children. To follow with an analytical mind the spontaneous remarks of boys and girls of any age will give an idea of the kind of stories to which they will respond, for the tales that are keenly enjoyed must reflect life that can be understood. It is simpler by studying conversations to get at the story interests of little children than of older ones, because small folk are more communicative than are those who are further on the way toward adult life. But even the adolescent youth, if his confidence is gained or his natural conversation overheard, will reveal, by his spontaneous remarks, tastes that indicate his story interests.

A science of story interests.—Because psychologists for many years have carefully observed children of all ages and noted their reaction to stories, we have come to have what may be called a science of story interests, and a set of rules that are a sure guide in choosing material. The one to be observed by the teller of tales to children of from three to six is, *use stories of which the characters are children, animals, parents, and personages like those that are part of the child's own life; tales that deal with the familiar.*

Stories in which there is a great deal of repetition and that contain jingles are amazingly popular during this early age of childhood. The response of little people to Mother Goose and kindred nursery rimes is proof of this statement. In fact, so keen is the enjoyment of tales told in rime or jingle that the years between three and six are often called the rhythmic period of childhood.

An eminent student of child psychology[1] declares that although the world at large is uncertain as to who Mother Goose was, the educational world knows she was a pedagogical genius. She understood the appeal of rhythm and alliteration for little children, and put her bits of narrative into a form that is received by them with delight. Whoever tells stories to tiny tots should bear in mind the appeal of Mother Goose, and introduce her principles as much as possible. even though he may not confine himself to that material.

Mother Goose discoursed about only those creatures and objects that are part of the little child's life. Mirth-provoking women and men, fat, good-natured old men, cross children and merry children, and amazingly wise animals fill her pages. They gambol and frolic, weep and rejoice, and have the kind of adventures that bring chuckles of happiness from the babes who hear about them. The story-teller who works with very small folks is certain of success if she keeps close to the methods of Mother Goose.

Jingle, rhythm, alliteration and rime.—Jingle and alliteration should be introduced into tales whenever possible, both for emphasis and for the purpose of feeding the love of sonorous sound that is very strong during the first five or six years of life. The mother or teacher who does not have enough literary ability to introduce into her work jingles that fit the material is heavily handicapped. Nevertheless she does not need to be discouraged. She can feed the love of rhythm that runs as high as that of rime, by

---

[1] *Centurion*, January, 1924.

repeating phrases and sentences to form stanzas, in the following manner:

> And so the birdie flew away,
> The birdie flew and flew and flew;
> The little birdie flew away
> Because God said cold days were near.
>
> In the sweet-scented garden of Eden,
> The beautiful garden of Eden,
> The pleasant green garden of Eden,
> Long ago there lived Adam and Eve.

Such bits as these, about a migrating bird, the paradise of Genesis, the sheep over which David watched, or the soft-eyed Baby Samson who became the man of strength, if introduced into a story, will greatly intensify the child's pleasure in the tale.

Repetition of conversation and descriptive phrase. —Repetition of conversation, or of descriptive phrase is also pleasing to little children. For instance, in giving the tale of a lark, very often, in speaking of the songster say, "And the wee little bird with the shiny, brown wings." Likewise, the account of a boy who was told to come straight home from the grocery when sent upon an errand, can be made more dramatic to the child, and the lesson one wishes to leave with him will be more deeply impressed, if one says, "His mother said, 'Come home just as fast as your bare feet can run, for we're going to have pudding for tea.'" Then, in recounting the incident where another boy tries to get him to come into his yard and spin tops, repeat, "But he remembered what his mother had said, 'Come home just as fast as your bare feet can run, for we're going to have pudding for tea.'" Make it a rule, when a message or principle is to be left with a little child, to emphasize that message or principle whenever possible by repetition and rhythm, even though rime may be out of the question.

Child's interest in parents simplifies acquainting him with God.—The fact that the little child is keenly interested in his parents, and in the parents of other children, greatly simplifies the work of the story-teller who seeks to arouse God-consciousness and awaken religious feeling. Through God, the loving Father, innumerable wonders are wrought. The world is his domain. Over it he presides as the earthly parent presides over his household, being mindful of those in his keeping, and doing for each and every one of them the thing that is best.

The parallel of the earthly and heavenly Father is very easy to establish with the little child because of his knowledge and belief in his own father. It is a comforting thought to him, in his awe of nature's forces, to learn that they move according to God's direction, and that within each one of them he speaks. Nothing else so gives such a sense of kinship with nature as does the feeling that the sun, moon, stars, light, darkness, thunder, lightning, and all else that is tinged with mystery are controlled by God, just as all creatures upon the earth are controlled by him.

The idea of Christ the Good Shepherd appealing to small child.—The idea of Christ the Good Shepherd is very lovely to the small child. He responds sympathetically to pictures and stories of shepherds whose business in life is to take care of the sheep. If he lives in a region where flocks move with the changing seasons in search of pasture, the sight of the sturdy men and dogs who tend them as they journey from lowland to hill country is one of keen interest to him. Having seen these taciturn, and usually foreign-tongued guardians, and heard them call to their charges, he understands the solicitude of shepherds for helpless animals.

If he is not in a sheep country, he will come quickly into an understanding of this solicitude if shown pictures of herders with their flocks. Rosa Bonheur's truthful and beautiful portrayal of a shepherd of the Pyrenees is splendid for this purpose. With it should be told the story of the lonely man who dwells in discomfort far from his kindred in the valley, because it is his business to care for helpless animals.

The account of the shepherds of Behtlehem who stayed abroad on the hills throughout the cold winter nights because to go to their home village would be to leave the dumb creatures to the mercy of the wolves, is a beautiful illustration of a guardian's care, and one that is loved by little children, if it is given picturesquely, with skill and sincerity.

God's care brought to the child through children of the Bible.—The children of the Bible are another medium through which God's care for his little ones can be brought home to the child. The tale of Baby Moses in the rushes, sheltered only by a basket of osier, yet unharmed by either river current or prowling beast until Pharaoh's daughter came down to bathe and took him to the palace, is a charming, appealing narrative for young children.

Appealing too are the stories of the birth of Isaac, of little Samuel, of young Joseph, who went to visit his brethren and was sold into Egypt. The tales of David, the shepherd boy, who became a king, of Samson, whose birth was the fulfillment of his parent's great desire, and of Ishmael, the child of Hagar, who languished with his mother in the wilderness, are among the most satisfying stories for little children to be found anywhere.

Much interest is aroused among small folk of from three to six by the story of Joash, the child sovereign of Judah, as told in 2 Kings 11, 12 and 13. The tale of little Mephibosheth (2 Samuel 4, 9), the crippled son of Jonathan, who was loved and befriended by King David, is another to which they respond with keen sympathy. Then there is the account of the baby Solomon, who grew to be a sumptuous ruler, and a man so wise that he could understand the language of all creatures. It is such Old Testament narratives as these, narratives that deal with children that are part of the young child's spiritual heritage.

The great animal story of the old Testament, the tale of Noah and the ark, is ideal for these small people. They listen eagerly to the account of God's care of the good Noah, to whom he gave warning of the flood, of the building of the ark that was to house him and his family throughout the weeks of deluge, and then of the gathering in of creatures of forest and field. The narrative of Noah and the deluge can well extend through several story periods, especially if as part of it, is given something about the various animals, and one or two of the legends clustering around them. Children of from three to six are much interested in hearing the old folk-tale of the dog who faithfully helped Noah to drive the many creatures into the shelter of the ark.

Then, when he attempted to get a place for himself, he found it so crowded that he had to stand half way in and half way out. Throughout forty days and nights the rain descended on his nose, at the end of which time it was so well-nigh frozen it never got warm again. Ever since that time dogs have had cold noses.

In the New Testament there is the crowningly beautiful tale of the infant Jesus, set in the background of a stable, with kneeling shepherds paying homage to the new-born Lord. The coming of the Magi, kings in sumptuous attire, riding on camels and bearing gifts from the farthest reaches of the desert, always charms and leaves a deep impression.

Sacred legends help in the child's religious training.—To supplement the story of the Christ-child there is a lovely Syrian legend of a baby camel that trotted beside its mother all the long miles across the waste, bleating in distress sometimes, and becoming so weary that the Magi had to stop and give its wobbly little legs a chance to rest. The children of Herod fed and decked it when the train stopped in Jerusalem. Finally, when the procession reached Bethlehem, it was left with the other animals while the three kings went to the manger.

But the wee camel, sensing that a glory was within that stable, succeeded in getting past the closed gate, beside which it had waited with its mother. It crept to the manger, and like the Magi, knelt in homage before the Child. The Child, seeing the bleating, adoring bit before him, raised a tiny hand as if in blessing. Then that baby camel went forth from the stable, never to be cross and vicious, like other camels, but to be happy and live forever.

To this day this revered legend is told around the firesides of Syria as part of the Nativity celebration. On Christmas Eve the little folks put dishes of pomegranate jelly and sweetened water outside their doors for the Baby Camel that walked to Jesus, that goes round the world each year on the Holy Night, leaving gifts for children, and even for adults who are sick and needy.

The story of the flight into Egypt is a charming one for young children, who are always greatly relived to find that Mary, Joseph, and the Babe get safely beyond the wrath of Herod.

This incident in the life of the Master can also be illuminated for folk of kindergarten and primary years by giving them some of the legends of the East. One of the most appealing of these is a tale that tells how, as the three hurried beyond reach of the murderous purpose of the ruler, they sought shelter one night at a gypsy camp. The chief let them stay by the fire, for although he knew who they were, and that the vengeance of Herod would fall upon him if he were discovered giving them protection, it was against the code of the wanderers to turn away anyone who was overcome by hunger, cold, or darkness.

The long, cold night wore on, and as hours passed the fire began to die out. The gypsies were asleep, and the strangers hesitated to rekindle it. The Child shivered with cold and the mother drew him close, but even so, she could not warm him.

High in a leafless tree above them was a small brown bird. It saw the shivering Babe and the half-dead embers, and flew down and fanned them with its wings. Into the very ashes it crept, spreading its tiny pinions and fanning incessantly.

Suddenly the embers flamed again, for wind from the moving wings of the robin revived some sparks. The fire burned merrily, as it had burned before, warming the circle where the gypsies slept, the wanderers, and the Child. But it blazed up so quickly that the breast of the bird in the ashes was sadly burned. Then God, because of the act of love and sacrifice of the small bunch of feathers, took the pain away. He declared that the scorched breast should be a mark of honor, so that evermore the world might know what one robin had done for a shivering Babe. That is why the gypsy mothers say robins have red breasts to this very day.

Another legend dealing with the flight into Egypt is that of a palm in an oasis in the center of the desert. It was an exceedingly tall tree, and proud as it was tall, because it had been planted by the Queen of Sheba, who, in the very long ago, had ridden to that oasis with King Solomon the Wise. She was returning to her own country after her visit to Jerusalem, and the sovereign and his train traveled part of the way with her. As they rested by a spring for refreshment from the long journey the queen said, "Here will I plant a date seed in memory of this hour, from which shall grow a palm that will live until a king greater than Solomon shall arise in Judæa."

She dropped the seed into the ground, and exactly as she had said, from it grew a palm such as that land never had seen before. Through many, many years it flourished, until now it was centuries old, yet still green and thrifty, like a fine young tree.

One day this haughty palm was approached by three human beings, a man, a woman, and a Child. The sun beat fiercely down upon them, and they were suffering from hunger and thirst. But never a sign of spring or green blade did they see. The man and woman dropped on the sand in misery, scanning the yellow stretches beyond with despairing eyes.

Suddenly, as they peered through the distance, they heard a rustle like that of wind in willows. Looking up, the woman saw the palm far beyond them, and dangling from its crown were pulpy clusters of dates. For a moment delight supplanted despair. The juicy balls would save them! She roused her husband. "See," she exclaimed, "dates that are pulpy and sweet!"

With hope revived they staggered close to the tree. But the fruit hung so high above that it was hopelessly out of reach. Faint from thirst, hunger, and much traveling as the man was, he could not climb the sheer shaft to where the bright clusters were. Despair possessed them again, but it was not so with the Child. He went close and spoke in a sweet, baby voice, "Palm, bend thee!"

Immediately a shiver went through the desert king. The tall, brush-like top lowered until it swept the ground.

Cluster after cluster of the pulpy fruit the child plucked. It fed and refreshed him. It fed and refreshed his parents too. When they all had eaten until satisfied, the little fellow spoke again, saying, "Palm, raise thee!"

The tree obeyed and the three passed on.

Next day, when travelers came that way by caravan, the leaves of the palm were seared and withered, for it had fulfilled its mission. A King greater than Solomon had risen in Judæa, and him it had sustained.

The story of the boy Jesus among the elders in the Temple is a lovely one for children of kindergarten and early primary years. There is also the beautiful narrative of Christ blessing the children, giving to them the time His disciples thought too precious to be devoted to small, insignificant folk. This is especially valuable in arousing in the little child that feeling of confidence and trust we desire him to have. To the wee tot, who often feels awed and helpless in the vast world that surrounds him, there is something highly comforting in the thought that the Master said, "Suffer little children to come unto me, and forbid them not."

THE INTERESTS OF OLDER CHILDREN

When the child comes to the age of six or seven his range of vision widens. He looks beyond his own fireside and the firesides of his neighbors, and to wonder about the world that stretches away out yonder and ever so far away. What kind of creatures inhabit it? What do they think, say, and do? Not being able to behold them in the flesh, he builds in his own mind images that fit his idea of them. Continually he is wondering, How does it happen that there are stars and a moon in the sky by night and a great yellow sun by day? Sometimes out of this wondering he evolves strange, grotesque theories. His imagination is awakened, and once awakened it knows no bounds. He now dwells in a realm of wonder peopled by giants, heroes, Indians, and other amazing characters.

The fairy-tale period of childhood.—This is the period of childhood when, like the winged horse Pegasus, imagination is a thing no man can control. Tales that satisfy now must be tales that feed the sense of wonder. During these years, which, broadly speaking, are from five or six to nine or ten, the craving is for narratives that abound in supernatural elements, those in which animals are endowed with human intelligence and attributes, and in which human beings perform feats that are impossible of achievement to mortals unaided, tales in which the happenings are such that only through the help of higher powers can they be brought about.

Numerous narratives in the Bible satisfy the demand for the supernatural.—The Bible has numerous narratives that satisfy the demand for the supernatural. The account of the serpent in Eden, of Eve swayed by its words and disobeying the command of God that had been spoken to Adam, of the two partaking of the fruit and hiding from the presence of the Lord when they heard his voice sounding among the trees, and then of being driven out of that beautiful domain into a place of thorns and thistles, is a fine example of a tale that feeds the child's craving for the supernatural. While satisfying that craving it establishes a sense of the power of God and the just punishment that came of disobedience.

The story of the creation, as told in the first chapter of Genesis, is a marvelous one for children of six and seven. Another wonder story from Genesis that satisfies to the uttermost is that of the visit of the angels and Lot's experience at the gate of Sodom. The building of the Tower of Babel and the confusion of tongues is still another.

The tale of Jonah, who fled from the presence of God and was swallowed out of the waters by a great fish, feeds the flight of fancy that is so well-nigh beyond control during these imaginative years. Incidents of the Exodus that satisfy this same desire are the account of Moses and the burning bush, the pillar of cloud and fire that guided the Israelites, the smiting of the rock when the wanderers were clamoring for water, the sweetening of the waters of Marah, manna rained from heaven, and the Red Sea waves rolling back to form a pathway for the oppressed and pursued Hebrews, but uniting again to destroy Pharaoh's destroying hosts. These and kindred narratives of the Old Testament, in which the workings of God are revealed in a spectacular and marvelous way, are not only enjoyed but needed by the child in this imaginative period. If his religious sense and belief in the omnipotence of God are to be established as we wish them to be, he must have a vivid sense of the sublime.

Failure to give wonder tales of the Bible while the child craves them often is followed by an irreverent or purely naturalistic attitude later on.—Skepticism and an attitude of levity toward the Bible often result when the wonder stories of the Book of Israel are presented to older boys and girls, who, because of the psychological period in which they happen to be, are unsympathetic toward them.

A lad of eleven came home from Sunday school scoffing at the account of Jonah.

"They can't fool me with that stuff," he declared.

His attitude toward a fairy tale or any other story involving the supernatural would have been the same. At the age of eleven most children have particular admiration for the heroic. They want tales of thrilling adventure—true stories as they say. Had this boy made the proper acquaintance of Jonah in the preceding years, instead of in this realistic period through which he was then passing, he could have received it with eager interest. He would have absorbed its lesson, just as he would have absorbed the lesson from Snow White and the Seven Dwarfs at a similar age, but might have laughed at it later. He was not old enough to have explained to him, without further shaking his faith in the Bible, that many tales found there were put into form by the Hebrew leaders for the sake of the truths they taught. Yet he was too old to accept the story without interpretation. Had he heard it while he was in the earlier stage of development, it would have aroused in him moods that would have made subsequent ridicule of it impossible. As it was, the parents could not correct the impression that the story of Jonah was ludicrous. He considered it an insult to his intelligence that somebody tried to make him believe it was so. He became skeptical toward all Bible tales because he had found one that was "a hoax," as he expressed it. From that time on he objected to going to Sunday school.

Taking into account the particular period of development.—No matter how spiritual or beautiful a narrative may be, or what ideals it embodies, *the child must make his first acquaintance with it in the period of his development when he craves material of that type, if it is to benefit him to the full limit of its possibilities.* Meat is wholesome food for the strong man, but to the week-old babe, who cannot chew and digest it, it would be starvation fare. Likewise, an athlete would turn in disgust from a diet of milk and rice water. It is the same with stories. A tale unsuited to a child in his particular period of development *is not a good story for him.* It brings him no message. It will not establish ideals or enrich his spiritual life. It may be even harmful to him, as was the tale of Jonah to the boy for whom its elements had no appeal. On the other hand, from the wisely chosen narrative, principles will be absorbed that become part of his code of belief and action.

The boy who at seven thrilled to "Jack and the Beanstalk" and learned the lesson of disaster evil-doing brings while he revelled in adventures in an enchanted region, never regards that tale as ridiculous, even though, as years pass, he grows beyond accepting it literally. It is the same with the Bible stories. The facts of some of them may be seen in a different light from that in which they were first viewed, but the spirit and symbolism of the tales, the religious feeling that was awakened in the child at the time of the initial hearing, will not depart from him.

Wonder stories of the New Testament.—The New Testament, as well as the Old, has much material that will be received sympathetically by children in the imaginative mood. The account of the appearance of the celestial hosts to the shepherds on the night of Christ's birth is very satisfying. The narrative of the star that blazed in the heavens and guided the Magi to the manger never fails to delight.

Very pleasing and nourishing also to children of this age are accounts of some of the miracles performed by Jesus, the multitude miraculously fed, the walking on the sea, and the calming of the waters, the eyes of Bartimæus opened, and the miraculous draught of fishes. In a word, whenever the supernatural enters into stories, if the characters and events are such that children of from six to eight or nine can understand them, they will respond eagerly to those tales and draw from them lasting impressions and truly spiritual lessons.

Wonder stories not the only ones children with active imaginations enjoy.—The question is sometimes asked, "Is one to tell only stories in which there is a supernatural element to imaginative children?"

The answer is, No. Children during this age are keenly interested in people. All individuals they can understand appeal to them now. But at this time, more than at any other, they live in a transcendent realm. Therefore Bible tales containing events possible only through superhuman forces mean more during this period than at any other. The child is in the same attitude of awe and wonder toward the mysterious as were his forefathers in the early morning of the world. The world teems with the mysterious and marvelous to him, and his attitude toward the marvelous is essentially religious. Later, when his belief in the unseen is not so strong, if he hears for the first time the wonder stories of the Bible, he will regard them dubiously, even sneeringly. Present-day scientific teaching tends to make older boys and girls scoff at miracle tales unless, when little children, they have received them as wonder stories and have caught from them the spiritual message they never fail to leave when belief in the miraculous runs high. This feeling of congruity for the truth they contain is a direct result of familiarity with them during the earlier years. Having heard these narratives during the early years of childhood, the attitude toward them is always reverent, even though, years later, a different interpretation is given them.

Summary.—During the early period of childhood children want stories dealing with familiar personages and creatures, stories, that reflect an environment with which they are familiar, or about which they have some curiosity.

Children in the later period of development, between the years of five or six and eight or nine, want tales that feed the imagination, fairy stories and narratives that abound in the supernatural.

Only during the particular period of development in which a story is inherently appealing does it influence life to the full limit of its possibilities. Therefore, the narrator should use great care in choosing material. His standards of selection are found in the experience of the group or of the individuals for whom they are intended.

THOUGHT QUESTIONS

1. Why is it necessary for the story-teller to understand the story interests of childhood?

2. What kind of stories should be chosen for children of kindergarten age, and why? Name some Bible stories that have an appeal for children of this age, and explain why they are appealing.

3. How does a little child's interest in his parents simplify acquainting him with God?

4. What are the story interests of children of primary years?

5. Are wonder stories the only ones liked by children in the primary department? Explain your answer.

CHAPTER V

THE STORY INTERESTS OF PRE-ADOLESCENTS AND ADOLESCENTS

As the years nine or ten are reached, the child emerges from the realm of fancy, so congenial to little children, into one of vigorous realism. His sense of reality or desire for "hard pan," is quite well developed. Fairy tales and stories tinged with the supernatural have lost their peculiar charm for him. For some time he has been asking the question, "Is it true?" He demands stories in which something happens, happens speedily, and the longer the sequence of lively events the better it pleases him. But all the happenings, according to his idea, must be possible. At this age he has a high regard for his intelligence, and resents what seems to him the insult of being told as a fact something he considers silly or improbable. He has reached the period of adventure. He longs to go to far places and have thrilling experiences, overcome wild beasts, sail the seas, capture pirates and fight savage tribes. The period of adventure has come.

HERO AND ADVENTURE STORIES

Boys and girls of from nine or ten to fourteen years yearn to migrate, to venture into new lands and claim them for their own. The actual physical experience being for the most part impossible to youth in this period, they get that experience vicariously. They *imagine themselves doing* the things they long to do, sometimes to the extent of telling wild yarns in which they themselves are the heroes, and to the dismay of their elders, who do not understand the cause of such fabrication and regard it as indicative of a tendency to lying.

This weaving of falsely fabricated stories sometimes happens during early childhood also, when parents and teachers are likely to be astounded by having some small John or Joan declare in all solemnity that he or she has witnessed or participated in happenings as grotesque and impossible as any of *Alice in Wonderland* or the Oz books. Yet the child is not meaning to lie. In his imagination the events really have occurred. His recounting them as facts is but a voicing of experience that is very real as he pictures it. If the adult to whom such incidents are recounted tactfully suggests that, of course, they did happen in the realm of make-believe, where anything may occur, he will usually find by the child's reaction that sincerity is the underlying motive in telling wild imaginings as actual occurrences. It was not a desire to deceive.

It is the same with children in the hero-worshiping period. Imagination does not take the grotesque flights it takes a few years earlier, but it is unceasingly active. In their desire for experiences they cannot actually have, boys and girls crave stories that are made up of adventure and deeds of heroism. Narratives that build character during these years must be those of heroism, of strong, fearless men and brave women who accomplish what the hearers themselves long to do.

The hero stories of the Old Testament.—Abraham, Isaac, and Jacob, whose stories, with that of Joseph, make up the great epic of the patriarchs, are fascinating personalities to young folk between the ages of nine or ten and fourteen. In the earlier periods they have had snatches about these men, bits here and there that, because of the nature of the incidents, had an appeal. Now these same characters should be seen as heroes of a great drama. Earlier in life, interest was focused on the forces that lay behind the various actions, the voice of God speaking to Abraham and the journey of the patriarch to a far country. Now there is eagerness to know what happened on the way. Adventure gives flavor to life during these years, and in using Bible stories it is necessary to remember that only as the boys and girls see the characters as heroes of a drama will they find them appealing.

Hero stories should be told in a sequence.—If the characters are to be seen as heroes of a great drama, it is necessary to carry them through the sequence of events that make up their lives. In this heroic period interest centers not so much on the children of Israel escaping the oppression of Pharaoh, as upon Moses, emancipator and lawgiver. Abraham, about whom very little was heard in the rhythmic and imaginative years, is a great personage now. Picturesque and splendid he seems to these older boys and girls, if shown as Genesis portrays him, a man of prosperity in Ur of the Chaldees, a chief who was almost a king in wealth and power, who might have lived on there in luxury had he been willing to worship idols instead of Jehovah-jirah, but who went forth into exile and to possible poverty and hardship because of loyalty to his faith.

The whole dramatic chain of events in the life of this patriarch is intensely interesting now. Young listeners follow him eagerly to the sojourn in Haran, where the old father died. In imagination they journey with him into Egypt to escape the famine that had become a grievous thing in the new country. With varying emotions they witness the parting of Abraham and Lot, the battle of the kings, Melchizedec's blessing of Abraham, the kidnaping of Sarah by Abimelech of Gerar, and the spectacular procession of sheep and oxen, man servants and maid servants, at the head of which the chief went to return the woman to her husband and to appease him for the wrong done in seizing her.

In this period, when love of adventure is such a vigorous emotion, adventure tales ring true for the same reason that age-old fairy tales ring true in the earlier period. These stories of the patriarchs satisfy even more than modern adventure tales, because young people sense without being told that they have grown out of the life of a people, and for that reason they touch deeper emotions than yarns spun by writers of to-day. Boys and girls feel the difference between these epics of Israel and twentieth-century "thrillers" exactly as the adult reader feels the difference between the tales of a man who has sailed before the mast and talks out of his experience and those of him whose knowledge of seafaring was picked up in a port town or on a single voyage. Intuitively, both old and young

distinguish between the genuine and the imi-
tative when it comes to stories. The adventure
narratives of the Bible always ring true. They
satisfy the adventure-loving spirit of youth.

**Leading boys and girls to see the different stand-
ards of life in different times.**—Episodes in the life
of the patriarchs—of all the Bible heroes, in fact—
that are hard to reconcile with the ethical standards
of to-day, can be accounted for without making the
heroes seem despicable, by explaining that customs
in those days were different from ours. Abraham's
treatment of Hagar seems more a fault of the times
than of the patriarch himself, if it is made clear
that a man was allowed as many wives as he chose,
and that a wife was the possession of her husband,
to be dealt with as he chose. In order to give
these old-time stories to young people without
dethroning the heroes in their eyes, or leading
them to condone their wrongdoing, it is necessary
to have them understand that, as the world ad-
vances, laws and social customs improve.

> "New occasions teach new duties,
>   Time makes ancient good uncouth."

What would make one a pariah in the twentieth
century was regarded as ethical when Israel was
young. This will explain also much of the revenge
and killing that splashed the lives of some of the
most high-purposed men of the Old Testament.
The law of an eye for an eye and a tooth for a tooth
held then.

The same principles apply to the presentation
of tales in which the fighting instincts and the baser
emotions are dominant—revenge, anger, and the

like. These are instincts of self-preservation, and crude men gratify them in a crude manner. But twentieth-century civilization demands that they be held in check. They should not be glorified in themselves. Wherever in the tales any of the base emotions are gratified with impunity from punishment, it should be made clear that men conforming to the highest ethical standards of their time were good citizens. But what constitutes good citizenship in one age may be crime when the world has advanced centuries beyond the standards of that age. Living according to the highest light one has is not sinful living. It is conscious law breaking or violation of the ethical or moral code of their day that stamps men as wrongdoers.

The tales of Isaac, Jacob, and Joseph are as appealing to adventure-loving boys and girls as is the story of Abraham. Like that of Abraham, these, too, should be told in a sequence. Then there is the great narrative of Moses, with its account of the long exodus toward the land that had been promised the Israelites. There are the red-blooded men of the books of Joshua and Judges, strong, elemental characters with both faults and virtues, so thoroughly human that children can understand them.

Joshua, the first soldier of the Hebrews, who routed the five kings, is a glorious character to adventure-craving youth. It is early in the story of the exodus that they first meet him, after Moses smites the rock of Horeb and the thirsting Israelites are refreshed with water. Amalek, grandson of Esau and chief of a tribe of Arabs, attacks the wanderers as they camp in the desert at Rephidim.

It should be made clear that this was a region of hostile tribes, who sallied forth ready to murder any one venturing into their territory or coming near it. Consequently, the Israelites were forced to fight for their lives.

It is here that Joshua is introduced, a youth who had come on the long migration and who had known all the horrors of slavery under Pharaoh. He was powerful, intelligent, brave, and loyal enough to his people to give his life for them if need be.

Moses knew the courage and devotion of this young man, and when the Arabians bore down upon them he spoke to Joshua saying, "Choose men and go out and fight with Amalek."

Joshua obeyed. At the head of the Israelites he faced the Bedouins and put them to flight.

Necessity of investing the Bible stories with color.—The necessity of presenting the Bible stories with all their natural picturesqueness and color cannot be over-emphasized. To say that the Israelites were attacked by a king whose territory they crossed is to give just a bare outline of this part of the story, and a very incomplete idea of it. But to make it clear that they were set upon by Bedouins, wild Arabs of the desert, a people who are intensely interesting to boys and girls, is to make the tale alive to them. With this episode should be told something of the ways of life of the Bedouins, and their history. That they are the descendants of Ishmael, the child of Hagar, is a very interesting discovery to young people.

Repetition of incidents that have been given as wonder tales or miracle stories.—The act of Moses holding up his hands, first of his own strength, then

aided by Aaron and Hur, and the success or failure
that came to the army of the Israelites according
to whether they were up or down, should be repeated
when the story of Moses and Joshua is given as a
hero tale. This incident, however, need not be
especially emphasized. In the primary period it
should be presented, not so much as a tale of Moses,
but as evidence of God's care of his people. The
thought of the power of Jehovah coming to the
army of the Israelites through the devotion of their
leader feeds the love of the supernatural that is so
strong at this age. It makes its greatest appeal
now. If during the imaginative period they have
had the account of the uplifted arms and have been
stirred to wonder and reverence by it, the repetition as part of the story of the great chief will give
them added pleasure and will stimulate unconscious belief in the God of the Hebrews.

From the time of the defeat of Amalek, Joshua
should be shown as the helper and support of Moses
until, in the valley of Bethpeor, God reveals to the
lawgiver the fact that the young man is to succeed
him, and on the plains of Moab the slave boy from
Egypt becomes leader of the Israelites.

Carry on the story of this great chieftain throughout its chain of events, with always the hand of God
strengthening him and enabling him to hold his
people together until, at the age of a hundred and
ten, he dies and is buried in the border of his inherit-
ance on the north side of the hill of Gaash.

The story of Joshua is such a splendid tale for
adventure-loving boys and girls, and so rich in
colorful incident, that no portion of it should be
omitted. To attempt to tell it in one story period

is merely to outline it. It should cover several periods, and can be used with advantage through nine or ten, if given against the rich background in which the children should see this hero.

The following is a good plan of presentation:

Part 1. Joshua Overcomes Amalek and Becomes the Helper of Moses. Exod. 17. 9–14; 24. 13; 32. 15–17; 33. 8–11. Num. 14. 1–45. Deut. 1. 38; 3. 28; 34, 9.

Part 2. God's Command to Joshua and the Crossing of the Jordan. Josh. 1; 2; 3; 4.

Part 3. The Siege and Destruction of Jericho. Josh. 5; 6; 7.

Part 4. The Siege and Destruction of Ai and the Reading of the Law. Josh. 8; 9.

Part 5. The Strife with the Five Kings and the Opposition of Jabin. Josh. 10; 11; 12.

Part 6. The Distribution of Canaan Among the Tribes of Israel. Josh. 13; 18; 19.

Part 7. The Cities of Refuge. Josh. 19; 20; 21.

Part 8. The Two and a Half Tribes Dismissed and the Altar of the Reubenites. Josh. 22.

Part 9. Joshua's Farewell and Death. Josh. 23; 24.

If the lesson plan of the Sunday school makes impossible the giving of the story of Joshua in so many parts, the narrator will necessarily have to condense and present the tale more in outline form than as an epic rich in atmosphere. The sequence, however, should not be broken. If, when the period of consideration of Old Testament stories is ended, the boys and girls do not see the various Hebrew leaders as great personalities who have done a definite work toward leading their people in the direction of well-organized civic life, they have missed much they should have gained. They cannot have this comprehension of the place of each of these men in the history of Israel unless they see them as heroes of a connected drama. If they are to catch the lesson of the life of Abraham, of Isaac, of Jacob, of Moses, Joshua, or David, they must behold each career in clear perspective. Those who study American history must see George Washington in order to understand the part he had in the upbuilding of our country.

Other splendid heroes for this period of adventure craving are Othneil, deliverer of the Israelites from the king of Mesopotamia, Ehud, Barak, Gideon, and Abimelech his son, Jephthah, the mighty man of valor, Samson and Micah. In the account of each of these a great deal happens, and from the standpoint of children it is all worth hearing about.

The Benjamite war is a mighty martial chronicle. Its recounting will hold the attention of young listeners to the point that they will be oblivious to all else but thoughts of the struggle that grew out of the days "when there was no king in Israel, and every man did that which was right in his own eyes."

In the books of Samuel and Kings are Saul, David, Solomon, and Jeroboam, each with a dramatic career from start to finish. Asa the good king, Ahab, who worshiped false gods and set up an altar to Baal in Samaria; Elijah, the righteous man of Gilead, who by his devotion to God worked miracles. There is the good reign of Jehoshaphat and the evil one of Ahaziah. Both of these are highly interesting stories, and so are the narratives of Joash, Elisha, and Hezekiah. The inva-

sion of Judah by Sennacherib and the siege of Jerusalem by Nebuchadnezzar the Babylonian complete the great cycle of hero tales that ends with the
second book of Kings. The Chronicles deal with
the same characters as those of Samuel and Kings,
and run parallel to them. Both renderings of the
narratives should be familiar to the story-teller.

On the whole, Solomon means more to adolescent boys and girls than to those in the earlier
period. He is a less crude and elemental character
than Joshua and the men of the first books of the
Bible. Therefore the older young people understand
him better. Parts of David's career also belong
in the adolescent period, and portions of the life
of Samson and Daniel. These parts are those that
have to deal with women, or that require a more
nearly adult understanding than that of boys and
girls of from ten to fourteen.

**Stories of heroism in first sixteen books of Old
Testament.**—The Old Testament material that
is especially suited to the needs of young folk who
respond to the heroic, is contained chiefly in the
first sixteen books of the Old Testament, omitting
Ruth. The story of Ruth in its entirety, like that
of Solomon, belongs in the adolescent period,
although scattered bits of it are interesting to
younger children. But the psychologist who has
gone deeply into a study of children's story interests doubts the wisdom of giving any portion of the
book of Ruth below the adolescent period. Even
though little children listen to it, it is not in the
early years that the benefit from this story is
greatest.

Material should be given in the period in which

it means most. The years of childhood are too few and too precious to fail to make the most of them by an unwise choice of narratives. In each stage of development a definite work is to be done, if the final result is to be intelligent God-consciousness, and a religious attitude of mind and heart that manifests itself in right thinking and living. The narrator needs to know his children as the painter knows the rules of color combination that enable him to produce a sunset or dawn at will. The blending of blue and yellow will not make red, and the giving to the child in the fairy-tale period the story of the early Christian martyrs will not cause him to respond with every fiber of his being to the courage that grew out of the mighty faith of these men. He will not catch the great message even though, as he listens, he thinks it very dreadful that good people had such treatment meted out to them.

The Age of Adolescence

The epic period of the child's life covers a longer range of time than any other. From the age of ten to eleven on through adolescence hero worship runs high, but it undergoes definite transitions. The lad at ten, and also at fourteen delights in living in a realm of stirring adventure, but his hero at the earlier age is a different type of individual from the one who awakens his admiration during the later. The man who conquers through physical prowess alone is his first ideal, he who is rugged and elemental. But, as he nears adolescence, a more refined type supplants this crude one. Deeds of spiritual courage and fine idealism arouse admiration. The youth who a little earlier valued muscular strength and skill above everything else now responds to tales of those striving for the victory of right over wrong, even though the situations abound in little physical exertion.

The early period of adolescence.—Between the years of fourteen and seventeen—the period varies with different individuals—life widens in unexpected ways. It widens rapidly and extensively, so rapidly and extensively that there is almost a sense of bewilderment in trying to keep pace with growing interests. Social interests are maturing. Boys and girls in this period are interested not only in heroic individuals, but they come into a consciousness of organized social interests. History appeals to them now, not only as a chronicle of men of achievement, but as a drama of nations, each one of which is a participant struggling to solve its portion of the problem of the world. Interest in interclass and international affairs begins to run high. Spontaneous debates and discussions as to social policies are carried on with deep earnestness.

A new sense of power possesses the boy or girl, a feeling of ability to overcome all obstacles, to cope with any danger. This feeling of resource sometimes far outbalances self-control, which also is rapidly growing now, but not rapidly enough to keep pace with the sense of ability to cope with any situation. Life is marked by an intensity of impulse, the impulse to do many different things—to do one, and then not to do it, but instead to do something that for the moment seems more glorious and exalted. Conflicting and sometimes impractical impulses they are, due to an effort to understand the rational foundation of life, and to find one's own place in life. These are years of passionate idealism, and tales of a very different type are needed from those that satisfy in the earlier period.

Saul of Tarsus overcoming in a struggle with himself and growing from a persecutor of Christians into the great apostle of the Christian faith is a more appealing hero now than David slaying Goliath.

Stories that satisfy during the first period of adolescence.—Highly satisfying to young people in the first period of adolescence are those that emphasize an ideal heroism, the account of a man facing death for a principle, or enduring suffering for righteousness' sake. The narrative of a boy true to a trust at a great physical or material cost to himself, but knowing the triumph of a satisfied conscience is deeply appealing now. Equally appealing is the chronicle of him who realizes a high ideal through great struggle and sacrifice. Such stories are received with sympathy because personal ideals mean much now. The ideals embodied in stories heard at this time affect the ethical standards of the boys and girls who hear them.

Tales that introduce individuals who are above the average physically are not without their appeal, but interest centers in the physical as a *means* to the realization of an ideal rather than around muscular strength itself. Such stories are especially enjoyed by boys and girls of athletic tastes. They are wholesome in their influence, especially if they embody high ethical ideals. They should have a place in the program of the narrator.

Tales in which men and women figure.—In the first period of adolescence interest begins to be manifested in tales that have both men and women characters. The lad in the preceding period cares nothing about girls and women in stories, except where they help his crude physical heroes to attain their ends. Between the years of ten and fourteen even girls turn from stories dealing with girls, if these tales do not abound in exciting incidents. They are interested in narratives that do not contain a single female character. They require stories filled with action and that satisfy a natural hunger for adventure.

Editors of magazines like Saint Nicholas say their greatest difficulty is to find girls' tales that girls of junior age like. Those in charge of children's departments of public libraries report that girls of from ten to fourteen read boys' books quite as much as those written for girls. Sometimes the number of boys' books taken out by girls exceeds the number of girls' books issued. Girls as much as boys in this period prefer adventure stories to every other kind of narrative. For this reason Bible stories dealing with men are more popular with juniors of both sexes than those containing women characters.

Deborah they admire because of her part in the defeat and death of Sisera, and the Witch of Endor interests them. But they are not interested in Mary anointing Jesus' feet. They can see no reason for that act, and regard it as foolish and wasteful. They do not understand that in her overwhelming gratitude the woman feels very humble. According to the junior idea the bestowing of a gift upon Christ would seem a better return for this service than anointing his feet. There is a poetic appeal in the Magdalene's act of devotion that they do not grasp.

When boys and girls reach the age of fifteen and sixteen, however, it is very different. Personal idealism and romance are then stirring in the soul, and the devotion expressed by breaking the box of ointment touches the deepest places of their nature. Stories that portray admirable types of both men and women are highly valuable now. They tend to foster wholesome thoughts in youths of both sexes and to create worthy ideals of manhood and womanhood. It is necessary that such ideals should be created in the time when sex feeling begins to awaken.

The later period of adolescence.—Between the ages of seventeen or eighteen and twenty-four transitions in the nature of the boy and girl are still taking place rapidly. They are not marked by such turbulence and intensity, however, as the ones that characterize the three or four preceding years. Sense of power is still a most dominant characteristic, of ability to render every situation subservient to desire. But youths of later teen age come slowly into a realization that there is a limit to their control over conditions, to their capacity for surmounting obstacles. Self-control is growing and strengthening. There is an increased social sense, and accompanying it, a growing respect for law. Not always is there conformity to law and the established order of things. Frequently independence, even defiance, is manifested in regard to prevailing opinion and belief. This is the outgrowth of desire for the expression of individuality and freedom from personal restraint. But recognition of the necessity of law as the foundation of the social order is present, even though particular laws are ignored.

Enthusiasm and aspiration are common traits. It is now that dream-houses are constructed and life plans are made. Careers are mapped out. Definite programs of personal achievement and success are formulated. Earlier, although dreams are dreamed and air-castles built, life is marked by conflicting impulses. A complexity of impulse tends to swing desire from one channel to another. In the first period of adolescence there are plans for the future, but on the whole they are not definite, fixed, certain. The later period of adolescence is characterized by fixed purpose and unswerving aim.

Independence, determination for self-assertion, dislike of restraint, a critical and sometimes cynical attitude toward adults—these are salient character-istics during the later period of adolescence, but they are tempered by a respect for law, a strength-ening of ethical feeling, by a quickened conscience, by lofty aspirations and wholesome, intense enthu-siasms. The story-teller who works with youth in this period has a tremendous opportunity for the strengthening of Christian character. By using stories that show how to overcome the self-assertive tendency that sometimes leads to disaster, and by choosing tales that direct enthusiasm and aspira-tion along wholesome channels, the narrator can be a splendidly constructive influence.

Stories for the later period of adolescence.—Of especial value during this period are tales that emphasize the necessity of devotion to social ideals and to the best social institutions. The need of this emphasis is especially great because of the tendency of many young people to disregard laws that interfere with their own pleasures and desires, even though they recognize the necessity of law as the foundation of the social order. Through stories that bring to them concrete examples of the fruits of misdirected passion and thoughtless independence, it is possible to overcome the tendency to shape their own course of action regardless of established laws and institutions.

During the later period of adolescence sex is fully awakened, and plays a vital part in the fixing of ideals and the formulating of life plans. It is therefore of great importance that young folk of this age have stories that teach the higher meaning of love, that portray clean, idealistic, but virile and buoyant manhood and womanhood. Many a person has carried perverted ideals through life, because of salacious stories heard and read during the days of adolescence. To fix in the mind and heart ideals that embody the higher meaning of love is not easy of attainment for the story-teller, but, except in the case of those with abnormal tendencies, it is within the range of his possibilities, provided he chooses material that is as strong in interest and as rich in human appeal as it is fine in ideal. But it must hold the human appeal, or it will not be received sympathetically. The telling of a weak story to adolescents is like scattering seed on a granite cliff. No growth will come from it. No enthusiasms will be quickened by it or resolves called into being. It will touch neither the emotions nor the life of those whose unwilling ears have listened to it.

THE BIBLE RICH IN STORY MATERIAL FOR ADOLESCENT YEARS

The Bible is just as rich in story material for the period of adolescence as for the earlier years. In the Old Testament there are characters who in some parts of their lives are highly interesting to boys and girls craving adventure, and even to the younger children, but whose appeal in other parts is to adolescents.

Samson, David, Solomon, and Daniel are chief among these. David slaying the Philistine and battling with Saul in the warfare that marked his reign is the hero of an adventure story of the kind juniors love. But David the stricken parent mourning for Absalom and David, psalmist of the Israelites, is of interest to the older group, those who have entered the period of romance. Samson the strong man and Samson the warrior should be introduced to juniors; but Samson betrayed and sent to his death by Delilah is a narrative for adolescents. So too with Solomon and Daniel.

Solomon enthroned in Israel in the place of Adonijah, who had exalted himself; Solomon the Temple builder and sumptuous ruler who maintained a court so splendid it was the talk of the world of that day and aroused the curiosity of Sheba's queen to find out for herself if rumors of its magnificence were true, is the hero of an exciting tale for twelve- and thirteen- year-olds. But Solomon who brought Israel to the pinnacle of her civic greatness, the man who established cities where before had been but open hill country and meadow land; Solomon, maker of proverbs and songs in adversity, is of interest during the later period.

For adolescents the story of Solomon should not end with his death. It should be understood that in making his reign one of unparalleled magnificence he put a heavy burden upon the people, one that not all his wisdom enabled him to see would make havoc in the land. When his son Rehoboam succeeded him, the oppressed subjects pleaded that he lighten the yoke his father had made so grievous. But this impetuous young king, refusing to be guided by the counsel of wise men who urged him to heed the voice of the people, threatened them with even a harder fate than the one they had known under Solomon, whereupon "Israel rebelled against the house of David to this day."

Daniel in the lion's den is a wonder story for children of primary age. When given as a continuation of the narrative of Belshazzar's feast and of the loyalty of a man to his faith despite the command of Darius, it is an adventure tale for those a few years older. But Daniel the man of vision, confession and prayer means most between the ages of fourteen and sixteen, and even later, when idealism runs high.

Many other characters and narratives of the Bible are like those mentioned above. In some portions they are nourishing food for little children, for juniors, or for both. In other portions they have a meaning only for adolescents. The story-teller can determine in which age they belong according to whether they are tales of miraculous happenings, adventure stories, or narratives of souls in conflict, or striving to realize high ideals; and whether or not they are tinged with romance that involves the two sexes.

Books of the prophets of interest mainly to adolescents.—Although scattered incidents from the books of the prophets are food for younger children, as a whole this portion of the Old Testament should be the story material for adolescents. The towering figures of Isaiah, Jeremiah, Ezekiel, and Daniel become men of great interest now. Boys and girls of this age should also meet Hosea, Joel, Amos, and the others who tell forth the meaning of the events in Israel. For the most part these are less spectacular characters than the major prophets, but they are men of great significance and human interest.

Characters of the New Testament of interest to adolescents.—The New Testament, with its narratives of Jesus and the apostles, is a treasury of stories for the years of adolescence. Matthew the publican, John and James, sons of Zebedee the fisherman, Simon and Peter, two other brothers who were fishers, Paul and Timothy and all of the disciple group are interesting, colorful personages to these near-adult folk. Individuals of mighty strength of purpose they were, simple, uncouth, and fearless almost to the point of being divine. The ministry and martyrdom of John the Baptist, the forsaking of his worldly calling by Matthew, a collector of taxes on goods crossing the Lake of Tiberias, to become one of the twelve, Peter's ministry and imprisonment, Saul's conversion and long pilgrimage in the cause of Christianity, and his final martyrdom at Rome, are incomparable stories for adolescents from the standpoint of their inherent, even if they had no spiritual value.

The women of the Bible interesting to adolescents.—It is during adolescent years that the women

of the Bible as personalities should be introduced.
During the rhythmic, imaginative and heroic periods
of childhood they are merely incidental to the outcome of the story. Now they become of interest
as human beings. And a goodly company there
is, even from the early chapters of Genesis. Not
all of them are as they should have been, but all are
interesting to those of the adolescent period. Their
lives carry lessons that need to be learned. Sarah
and Rebecca, Deborah, Athalia, Hagar, Jezebel,
Bathsheba, Delilah, Ruth, Naomi, Esther, Martha,
Mary Magdalene and the other Marys, women of
the Old Testament and women of the New, all are
characters that budding men and women should
know. Ruth, a maiden of the gleaners, and Esther,
the captive Jewess who became queen of Persia,
are especially appealing, and, as examples of high-
souled womanhood, their histories are conducive
to the establishing of high ideals. The beautiful
love tale of Ruth and Boas is wholesome and stim-
lating. This and other outstanding love stories
of the Bible, the narrative of Isaac and Rebecca,
and all the others of the same type that the Old
and New Testaments hold should be as familiar to
young people of later teen years as is Mother Goose
to little children. The incidents themselves are
intensely interesting and when the characters are
presented against the vivid, colorful background
that made up their native environment they are
unequaled among the great love stories of the world.

The crowning narrative of the Bible.—The sublime
narrative of the New Testament is that of Jesus of
Nazareth, from whose lips came a creed of brotherhood that will regenerate mankind. His baptism by

John the Baptist, the Sermon on the Mount, the refuting of the Pharisees, his calm, understanding answer when he was despised in his own country, his entry into Jerusalem, his parables and miracles, his unceasing toil to uproot hatred from the hearts of men, and his voluntary death on the cross— these constitute the greatest story of the ages both spiritually and as a work of literature. Given adolescent youth as it should be given, with the Master the central figure of a sublime drama, it will bring the finest and deepest emotions into activity. It will arouse feelings that cannot be expressed. Considered solely as a story it is the most superb epic known to man. This fact, combined with the one that it is the world's supreme religious document, makes it the tale of tales for the awakened heart and soul. All the God-consciousness, high faith and consecration of Christianity we dream of for flowering youth can be brought about by it, provided it is given by one whose skill in presentation, whose reverence and whose own faith are such that, as it falls from his lips, it loses none of its mighty spiritual appeal.

Summary.—Four distinct types of story-interests fill the child's life. The little child wants tales of personages like those that are part of his world.

Following this first period he lives in a realm of make-believe. He delights in stories whose characters are fantastic, supernatural creatures, or those in which events occur that are possible only through the work of supernatural forces.

Then there is a craving for true stories, tales of heroes, of youth and manhood on the path of adventure, triumphing through physical bravery.

Finally, stories of high idealism are desired, those in which spiritual courage more than physical is the moving force, or in which physical prowess is a *means* to the realization of a high ideal. Tales especially needed now are those that foster respect for established laws, worthy institutions, and accepted principles, that emphasize self-control, and that teach the higher meaning of love and service.

THOUGHT QUESTIONS

1. Describe the story interest of children of from ten to twelve.
2. What portion of the Bible is particularly valuable in working with adventure-craving children?
3. Why is it important that we give children an idea of the various standards of life in different periods of history?
4. Should incidents in the life of Moses, Joshua, etc., that have been given as wonder tales in the imaginative period, be repeated in the period of adventure? Why and how?
5. Prepare the story of Joshua to give in nine chapters.
6. Prepare the above named story to give in two chapters.
7. How many periods constitute the age of adolescence? Define characteristics of each, and explain story-interests of each.
8. Mention some Old Testament men and women who are of particular interest in the age of adolescence.
9. What is the crowning narrative of the Bible for those of adolescent years? Mention six New Testament characters beside Christ who are of particular interest during adolescent years.

CHAPTER VI

HOW STORIES CAN BE USED

MORAL and religious training should begin in the cradle. Systematic instruction along ethical and spiritual lines should commence as soon as the child begins to manifest an interest in things around him.

In many homes religious training does begin then, but it is not always systematic. The mother is sometimes uncertain as to the method of procedure, or she may think the child too young to be put through a definite course of training. Usually, scattered bits of Bible stories are given to these tiny tots, and not infrequently the ones chosen are unsuited to their understanding. Sometimes they are told abstract truths that again they do not understand.

In many homes in which a serious attempt is made to give religious instruction, babes of three and four are informed that God is the great father who created all things, and therefore they must love him. They are urged to love Jesus because he was the Son of God and died to save the world. The result is that the small boy or girl is bewildered. He has one father. The idea of another puzzles him. The thought of Christ dying to save the world is too weighty for him to comprehend. The little mind is in a state of confusion. Very often, by the questions and remarks of these wee learners, parents discover that the teaching is not obtaining the results for which they had hoped. They conclude that leading young children into the highway of religion is a very difficult matter. Under such conditions it is natural for them to infer that children are not ready for systematic spiritual training before the age of six or seven.

This is a mistaken idea. To give the tiny child a foundation upon which a splendid spiritual structure can be built is not difficult. As soon as he can understand Mother Goose he can also understand brief, simply told stories about God and his creatures, and be deeply moved by them. But there will be no quickening of activity in his emotional life if he hears the abstract statement that God created all things and therefore he must love him. He must have a picture of God as a Creator and Father. He must think of the heavenly Father as wonderful, thoughtful, and kindly if his response is to have educational value.

The Training of the Young Child

The man or woman who, as a little child, has *felt* God as the great, protecting Father, never wholly loses a sense of trust in him. Children may *hear about* God, and may be taught the Christian conception of God without ever coming to have a personal knowledge of him. But to feel him in the world that surrounds them is to *know* him. To have a vital knowledge of God is to come into a sense of harmony with and trust in him that can never be entirely lost. *It is the business of the religious teacher to bring children into this imme-diate, vital knowledge of God.*

God most effectively introduced through nature.—
The most effective way in which to introduce God
to the little child is through nature. Take him into
a garden some day among the birds and flowers.
If a visit to a garden cannot be arranged, show him
a picture of children in a beautiful garden scene,
or one of flowers, of birds in flight, drinking at a
fountain or bathing in the dust. Then tell him that
ever and ever so long ago there were no birds, no
flowers, no little boys and girls, no fathers, no
mothers, no animals. There were no pretty brooks
running down from the hills, or springs where people
could drink when they were thirsty. There was no
sunshine and no light. Everything was black as
the darkest night. It was even blacker than that,
because there was no moon to shine, and no twin-
kling stars to light up the darkness. There was
only God, and he was so great and powerful he
could do whatever he willed.

God wanted things to be beautiful, good, and
happy, so he said, "Let there be light!"

And light came, because God made the great
round sun to shine by day. He made the moon
and stars to brighten the night. He made hills,
valleys and rivers, pretty brooks and springs. He
made trees and flowers too—everything on the whole
beautiful earth.

From this beginning it is easy to lead to the creation of animals and man. Having God the Creator
introduced in story form, the child is able to understand God the Father. Because of the approach
through familiar things—the flowers and birds that

he knows, the sun, moon, and stars that have awakened his curiosity, and the people that are part of his life—he sees him as the father of all creatures, of his own father and mother, his grandparents, every one in fact. Thus in the awakening mind reverence begins to find a place and a system of causation is established.

Little children need very short stories.—Workers with children of three and four should bear in mind that these small folk can comprehend only very brief, simple stories. To try to hold the attention with one tale for more than five minutes is a mistake. No matter how interesting it may be, concentrating upon a theme for more than five minutes is a tax upon the mind of the young child that results in lack of interest. When this occurs the value of the story period is lost. If hearers are either physically or mentally weary, the message of the narrative is not deeply impressed upon the mind. Fifteen or twenty minutes a day of stories may be minutes of happiness to babes of three, four, and five, but between tales there must be periods of activity—a romp in the sunshine, a song or march if it be in the Sunday school or kindergarten, or in the home on a rainy day. If there is a supply of bird and flower pictures much benefit and pleasure will come of cutting and pasting some of these after the creation story has been heard.

Value of the sand-box to those who tell stories to little children.—A sand-table or box may mean so much to whoever tells stories to little children that every home, kindergarten, and Sunday school should be provided with one. It is within the reach of even the poorest home, because if no other equipment is available, there can always be obtained a large wooden box, the sides of which can be cut down to convenient height. Newspapers under and around it afford protection to carpets and rugs if it must be placed in a dining or living room. Even if conditions prohibit keeping such a box indoors always, the value and pleasure to the child of playing stories in the sand make the effort of moving it in and out, or of emptying and refilling it worth while. A sand-pile in the backyard is a priceless asset to the home in which there are little children, but when weather conditions make out-of-door play impossible there should be a sand-box in the house.

Following the account of the creation the small child can work out the narrative in sand. He can model mountains and plains. Pieces of blue paper or bits of a broken mirror will serve as rivers, lakes, and seas. Catalogues of florists will supply flowers for gardens and the magazines are filled with pictures of children, animals, and birds. The religious leader who supplements the story periods with periods of cutting and pasting pictures, or of sand play, will accomplish far more than the one who uses no such aids. The child's expression of the story in his own crude way is of almost as much benefit to him as the hearing. In working it out he continues to relive it. Its message becomes indelibly stamped upon his mind and heart.

Long narratives as cycles or groups of short ones. —For three- and four-year-old children the account of the creation should be broken into several parts; that of the making of the world, sky, stars, moon, darkness, and light being one chapter in the cycle, that of the creation of animals a second part, while that of man makes a third.

Each chapter told should be constructed as an independent story. In breaking a narrative into several parts it is necessary that each portion be told in such a manner that the rules of story structure are observed. In other words, the various events should be arranged in such a manner that they contribute to a definite climax. In the first part of the story of the creation the flooding of the world with light that follows the making of sun, stars and moon is the climax.

In the second part emphasis should be placed upon the coming of the many animals upon the earth, little creatures of the woods and fields, fowls and birds that fly "in the open firmament of heaven," small, four-footed beasts, great quadrupeds of the land and whales of the sea, until finally there was "every living creature that moveth."

In the third and last portion of the account of the creation, where man is formed in the image of God, the climax lies in the making of Eve to be the companion of Adam.

Leading from the smaller to the larger, from the lesser to the great, is what gives climax to a story. If this fact is remembered and each chapter is constructed with a view to climax, the tale is certain to be satisfying to the child, provided it is well told.

Stories should be retold frequently to little children.—Every time a child hears repeated a story that has been enjoyed, he re-experiences the emotions that were his when he first heard it. At each hearing its lesson or truth becomes more deeply impressed upon his mind and heart. Therefore there should be frequent repetition of stories. So long as the child manifests pleasure at the recounting of a tale it is good for him to hear it retold. As long as he says, "Tell it again," and his eyes kindle with pleasure as the narrator begins it, his emotional nature is growing while listening to that story. He is experiencing moods that stimulate and enrich his personality.

But once he shows the least lack of enthusiasm as the tale begins, or asks for something different when it is suggested, it should not be repeated. That particular narrative has served him as much as is possible in that stage of his development. To repeat a story after a child has begun to tire of it is to antagonize him, the thing above all others the story-teller should avoid.

In the kindergarten, church school, settlement house, wherever an attempt is made to instil and nurture religious feeling in the small child, the same principles hold. Give tiny tots brief, very simple stories, and tell them again and again, as long as interest in them runs high. This does not mean that one narrative should be given day after day to the exclusion of all others. Give the account of the creation of the world, of animals, of man and the first parents in the garden, and several others if that procedure best fits the mood of the teller. But do not present these narratives once only. Keep traveling back along the road that has been covered. A small child needs to hear the same story several times before he absorbs from it all that he is capable of absorbing.

The Story in the Program of the Home and Church School

Broadly speaking, the story should be part of each stated period of religious training of children. Below the period of adolescence it should have a place in every session of the church school, and that place should not be a minor one. During the period of adolescence it should also have a place, though a less prominent one. There are types of lessons that do not require the use of the story. Especially is this the case where argument, logic, historic or scientific accuracy are to be stressed. But even between the years of eighteen and twenty-four, and in adult classes, the story is a powerful aid in emphasizing truth and impressing it upon the mind. On the whole it is the most effective means of aiding the memory of church school pupils. It should be used freely, although it is not necessarily a part of *every* session in the secondary division.

But it *is* a necessary part of the program of every religious session with young children. During the first six or seven years there should be a religious tale in the home every day or evening. This seems an impossibility to the busy mother; but if desire to enrich the child's soul is great enough, it can be accomplished, and without great sacrifice. A few minutes will suffice to draw from the Bible the brief narrative a little child should have, and the fact that the same stories should be repeated several times simplifies the task. When the babies are put to bed a few minutes more can be devoted to the retiring time, enough in which to give them a brief, nurturing tale. Children love good-night stories.   The bedtime story too, of the mother who wishes to inspire a God-consciousness in her children, should be the old, old Book that has food for every taste and every age.

Mothers and teachers should be good story-tellers.—Because of the supreme place of the story in the religious education of children, it is highly important that the mother be a good story-teller. In fact, when one considers what are the most abiding influences during the years of childhood, it can be said that she is not a wholly efficient mother who does not give narratives to her children.

It is equally necessary that the church school teacher in the elementary grades be a good story-teller.   The most important item of his mastery of method lies in the field of oral narration.   He should know the Bible from beginning to end as a storybook, and be able to put into its tales as he tells them the essence of his own faith.   All his own God-consciousness must be reflected in the narratives he gives, if a like God-consciousness is to be awakened and sustained in the minds of his pupils.

Stories from supplementary sources.—The worker in the religious field should know many stories besides those drawn from the Bible.   Numerous tales outside the Testaments are essentially religious and put the child into moods that enlarge his faith and foster spiritual growth.   For the most part these are nature stories and primitive wonder tales. Narratives of this type help to make the Bible tales more vivid.

Suppose, in the Beginners' Department of the church school—or in the home—the lesson is on

God's love and care of all creatures. A nature story like the following will make love and care clear.

THE GREAT FATHER AND THE BIRDS

"The creatures God made when he created all things were very different in their looks. The sheep is not like the horse. The pig is not like the bear, and they are as different in the things they do and the way they live as in their looks.

"Some of them are strong and happy in cold weather, while others need warm, soft days. The big white bear must have ice and freezing water. If he does not have them, he will die. But God takes care of that. He has put the white bear away up in the cold north country, where there is everything he needs to keep him well and strong.

"The robin that sings and twitters throughout the summer gets very cold when freezing weather comes. He cannot live in a land of ice and snow. So, before God sends winter he tells robin to fly far, far away to a country where there are no snow-storms, where the days and nights are always pleasant. Because little robin knows how well God cares for him he does as he is told. Away to the sunny south he travels, and sings happily there until spring comes. Then God lets him know it is time to go back, and joyfully he spreads his wings and flies home.

"Many other birds are like the robin. They go south when the frost comes and fly back in the spring, because God tells them where to go in order that they may be safe and happy."

The account of the migration of the birds can

be one of a cycle of tales illustrating God's care of the animals, another chapter of which can be built around the squirrel laying up winter supplies because the Great Father has taught him that unless he does he will starve. The account of the bear hibernating in caves and the hollows of great trees because God has shown him that is the way of preservation also holds much interest in this early period. It emphasizes in the child's mind the thought of Omnipotent care for every creature.

Teaching lessons by Bible stories in early childhood.—In the period when the love of fairy stories and miracle tales runs high, the account of the Children of Israel oppressed in the land of Egypt and delivered from the cruelty of Pharaoh is a fine illustration of God's protecting love and care. This story should be told very simply, not as to boys and girls in later childhood, with emphasis upon the acts of Moses and Aaron and an attempt to show them as great personages, but as a narrative of God caring for those who needed his protection, in terms a little child can understand. The following rendering illustrates the point:

GOD SAVES THE CHILDREN OF ISRAEL

A long, long time ago there were some people called Children of Israel who lived in a land beside a great river.

Egypt was the name of that land. It was a beautiful country, with broad, sweeping plains that were the color of gold, and great houses painted from top to bottom with wonderful pictures. But the Children of Israel were not happy there. A

wicked king ruled over them and made them work
as his slaves.

Slaves are people who have to work for other
people and never get any pay for their work. They
have no good homes, but must live in dirty old
sheds, in caves in the ground, or any place they
can find. And they never have enough to eat.
But no matter how hard things are for them, they
must go on living in the same terrible way, because
as long as they are slaves they belong to the man
they work for, and he will not let them go away.
The king who held the Children of Israel as slaves
was called Pharaoh. He did many dreadful things
to them. He made them work so long and hard
without stopping that some who were not very
strong fell down dead.

It was all very terrible, so terrible that the women
and children, and even some of the big, strong men
cried. They could not sleep at night because they
were so tired and aching from the hard, hard work.
If they did not get up early in the morning and
begin working with all their might, Pharaoh's soldiers would come and whip them.

The Children of Israel were good people, and
God did not want them to suffer so. He told them
to go away from Egypt to a land where they would
be free and happy, where they might work for themselves, and not have to be slaves of a cruel king.
He said he would show them the way.

Now it happened that among the Children of
Israel was a wise and good man named Moses—
before beginning this story, if children have not
had the account of Moses in the rushes, it should
be told to them—the very same Moses who, when

a tiny baby, was found by the princess among the rushes by the river. Moses had grown not only into a wise and good man, but into one who was very brave and strong, so God said he should be their leader.

Moses gathered the Children of Israel together, and they went out of the country where they had been so sad. It was a long, hard way over desert and mountains, but steadily and gladly they trudged along toward the land God had promised them, until they came to the shore of the sea.

When Pharaoh found that the Children of Israel were gone he was very angry. He wanted to keep them in the land of Egypt to build houses and dig ditches for him, and to do many other things. So he called his soldiers and said: "Come with me, and get the Israelites back. I will not let them go away."

Very quickly the soldiers obeyed. They brought the king's chariot, a little two-wheeled wagon painted in bright colors and trimmed with gold. All kings rode in chariots when Moses lived, for in that ever and ever so long ago there were no carriages or automobiles. The soldiers hitched horses to this chariot; splendid, swift-footed horses that could go like the wind.

The soldiers had chariots too, and as soon as the king was ready they hitched horses to their own. Then away they all went, the soldiers behind Pharaoh, an army of six hundred in all.

They whipped their horses to make them go faster and faster. They dashed across plains covered with yellow sand until they came to mountains where the rocks were so sharp and high it took a long, long time to get over them. But finally they got up one side and down the other. Then, as Pharaoh looked ahead, he saw Moses and his people going toward the promised land.

When the Children of Israel saw Pharaoh's army hurrying after them they were very much afraid. The sea was just in front so they could not go forward, and they knew if the soldiers overtook them, they would have to go back to the land where they had been so unhappy. Some of them cried out in fright and covered their faces with their hands.

But God did not mean to let them become Pharaoh's slaves again. He spoke to Moses, and said, "Lift up thy rod, and stretch out thine hand over the sea, and divide it; and the Children of Israel shall go on dry land through the midst of the sea."

The rod was the staff Moses carried to help him in walking over rough places. He lifted it up and stretched it over the sea, as he was told.

Then a wonderful thing happened. The waters parted and made a broad, dry path. It was so dry it would not wet even a piece of paper. The Children of Israel went by this dry path across the sea and came safely to the other side.

"Look," the soldiers cried as they watched the wonderful thing happen, "the Israelites are passing between the waters."

Pharaoh was terribly angry when he saw that Moses and his people were getting away from him.

"Follow and overtake them," he shouted. And away he went after the Israelites.

The army in the chariots started across the sea

by the broad, dry path, and again the poor people were very much afraid, for as they looked back they could see the king and his soldiers getting nearer and nearer. They were sure now that they would have to go back to the hard, sad life in Egypt.

But once again God spoke to Moses.

"Stretch out thine hand over the sea, that the waters may come again upon the Egyptians," he said, "upon their chariots and upon their horses."

Moses stretched out his hand as he was told. The waters of the sea came together and covered the path. The king and his soldiers were drowned. Not one of them was ever seen again. But God protected the Children of Israel, and they went forward on their way.

In this period of early childhood, the story of the Exodus with its many miraculous happenings makes a delightful cycle of tales, or a two- or three-part narrative. The specific manner of presentation depends upon the plan of the course under which the narrator works and upon his own mood. If given as a two-part story, the first would cover the oppression under Pharaoh, the commissioning of Moses to deliver Israel, and the plagues of Egypt, as related in Exodus 1–12; the other dealing with the departure and events on the way, the pillar of cloud and fire, the destruction of Pharaoh's army, etc. If given as a cycle, each of the miracle episodes can be worked into a separate story, as illustrated above in the account of Pharaoh's army. The point is, the wonder tales of the Bible should be used to the limit of their possibilities in the period when love of such narratives is strongest.

The use of pictures illustrating Bible stories and truths.—Much emphasis should be placed on the use of pictures by the story-teller. When well chosen they can be of great benefit and pleasure to the child. Much of the greatest artistic genius of the world has gone into the illustrating of biblical stories. Michael Angelo, Titian, Raphael, Velasquez, Botticelli, Murillo, Rubens, Van Dyke, Durer, and a host of other masters gave the very flower of their talent to portraying happenings in the Old and New Testaments. Whenever it is possible to obtain them, suitable pictures from this vast wealth of art treasures should be used. Print reproductions of masterpieces that can be obtained for as little as a penny and that help to make the stories vivid are within the reach of every church school and almost every home.

The method of using pictures varies with the mood and plan of the story-teller. They may be introduced into the telling of the story. Sometimes it is best to have them precede the telling of the story, the story itself growing out of the picture, or they may follow the telling. After hearing a tale, children enjoy studying a picture that illustrates it. They like to find the characters in it, and visualize portions of the tale that the picture does not touch. So long as there is a *definite purpose* in the mind of the narrator in using pictures, the time and method of using them is largely one of personal taste. The skillful story-teller sensing the response of the class, will use pictures to fit conditions, just as she uses the story material.

The use of poems and songs.—Poems and songs that emphasize God's care may also be used freely.

It is important also, in working with little children, that the story-teller draw with a lavish hand from the nature myths and animal and plant legends that carry beliefs about origins. These are highly religious narratives to the little child, because they put him into moods in which he feels omnipotence in nature. They enrich his emotional life.

The following poem will illustrate what is meant:

THE LEGEND OF THE FORGET-ME-NOT

When to the flowers so beautiful
　　Our Father gave a name,
Back came a little blue-eyed one,
　　All timidly it came.

And standing at the Father's feet
　　And gazing in his face,
It said, in soft and gentle tones,
　　And with a modest grace,

"Dear God, the name thou gavest me,
　　Alas, I have forgot!"
The Father kindly looked on her,
　　And said, "Forget-me-not!"

Stories should be told to children, not read to them.—The plan outlined above will be suggestive to the teacher as to the manner in which to use the story. No matter what theme is the basis of the lesson, the children should be interested in it through the medium of the story. The lesson sheets tell the church school worker where to find the Bible story. Those prepared by some denominations give a retold version. When this is done the teacher should then study that story until he can tell it well. *It should not be read.* Stories lose half their effect when read, because then the attention of the teacher is divided between the children and the printed page. In order that the child shall receive the full message and experience the joy that should be part of the hearing, a tale must be given with spontaneity and enthusiasm. This is impossible when the mind and eye of the narrator are following the printed lines.

Reading from the Bible should be a part of the religious-education program with older children and adolescents, but the oral telling of the story or part of the story preceding the reading sometimes is needed to help interpret what is read. Anyone who has been a college, or even high-school student of English knows why this is so. A famous American teacher of literature attributes much of his success to the fact that he has been a generous user of the story with his classes. In the study of a novel or short story he prefaces assignment and discussion with enough of an account of the narrative itself to arouse interest concerning it. The result is a reaction on the part of students that yields gratifying results.

Bible stories should be prepared from the Bible itself.—If the Bible story is not told in the lesson leaflet, the teacher herself should prepare the narrative according to the principles of story structure already considered, and tell it to the children to the best of her ability. But whether a retold account is at hand or not, she should read the Bible version so as to get the feeling or tone of the Bible. Although for many years artists have been writing

Bible stories, the world has yet to see one that equals the original either in spiritual or literary beauty. The only reason for attempting to retell these incomparable tales is because they are given in language and style that is not the everyday speech of our time. The purpose of retelling is not to attempt improvement, but to give a better understanding than would result if they were presented in the original form, and because the appeal of the spoken tale is greater than that of the printed one.

The story a part of a varied program with older children and adolescents.—With children having the spirit of adventure, and also with adolescents, the story may be used in a program of poetry, song, and discussion. But just as with the younger people, the oral telling of the story should precede discussion. Such a method tends to stimulate interest throughout the whole hour. There are class leaders so admirably equipped for their work that by skillful questioning they can immediately arouse interest in almost any subject, and lead up to the story in such a manner as to heighten delight in the tale. But the worker of average ability and limited training will find it easier and safer to let questioning and discussion of the theme follow the story. Genius can break all rules without disastrous results. But the beginner in the field of religious education, or the worker who is feeling his way, will be wise not to disregard them.

Bible reading and story-telling.—Much Bible-reading should go hand in hand with the oral telling of the story when the work is with older boys and girls, partly that the teacher may absorb the loveliness of the language and style of the Hebrew narrators, partly that he may drink deeper of the messages the pages hold. For instance, follow the account of the narrative of the exile of the Jews with a reading of the one hundred and thirty-seventh psalm. After hearing about the misfortune of the chosen people, that song of sad recollection will be listened to with deep sympathy. In a word, everything that will help to make the Bible alive and interesting to the child should be considered in connection with the lesson. The teacher should try to reproduce in them the attitudes of the Hebrews when these stories emerged from their lives. It can be done. If it is not done, the narrator fails to make the most of his opportunity.

Pageantry, dramatization, essays and debates.—
When working with pupils of adolescent years, it is sometimes advisable to use the stories as themes of essays, debates, pageants, and dramatization. In connection with this last suggestion a word of caution is necessary. Unless the teacher has sufficiently mastered the material to have it at the fingers' ends, it is not safe to attempt dramatization. Uncertainty on the part of the leader will breed disorder and disaster. But if the stories are as familiar as the multiplication table, so that by a word here and a suggestion there the youthful players can be guided whenever in need of help, much benefit will come through dramatization.

Several publishing houses issue in drama form, Bible stories suitable for boys and girls in all grades. A list of the same is given in the chapter dealing with sources of material. But before going into the dramatized version, the narrative should be thoroughly familiar to every member of the group.

Pageantry and dramatization should be an expression of religious feeling.—If dramatization or pageantry are attempted, great care is needed on the part of the leader that boys and girls do not regard it as putting on a show. It should be an expression of religious feeling by those who have a part, and unless undertaken in this spirit should not be attempted. The right attitude toward this type of work can usually be created by giving an account of the origin of the Passion Play of Oberammergau and other religious dramas that have been produced for centuries by peasants of the old world, each one of which has been an expression of reverence and gratitude rather than the desire to produce a spectacle.

The Passion Play of Oberammergau came about almost four hundred years ago, when a plague swept the little village in the Bavarian mountains and threatened to depopulate it. As the people prayed for deliverance they vowed that if God would stop the ravages of the disease, they would, every ten years from that time forth, portray the passion and crucifixion of the Saviour as an act of thanksgiving to him.

In that spirit, almost since the days of Columbus, with but just a few exceptions due to war or conditions beyond their control, these simple artisans have produced their religious drama as reverently as ever men and women knelt in a church. Never has it been given as a show in the hope of having an audience. Its enactment has been a prayer of gratitude, with every one in the village taking part. Gradually peasants in neighboring villages came to attend the observance in the same spirit as

people from one town go to church service in another
town.   Then the world beyond the highlands heard
about the Passion Play, and within the last century
there has been an exodus from all over the world
to Oberammergau, not because the people themselves advertised and tried to draw the multitude,
but because desire to see the reverence of these
peasants sent them there of their own accord.

It is well to make clear to the boys and girls what
participation in the Passion Play means to the folk
of Oberammergau.   From childhood they try to
live in such a manner as to be worthy of a part in
the great religious observance.   It is the goal toward
which they continually strive, and the only hope
of reaching that goal is by walking in the path of
righteousness.   Like theirs, the attitude of all who
participate in religious dramas should be one of
reverence.

**The use of sacred legends in the adolescent
period.**—The teacher of adolescents should supplement the Bible stories with tales from other sources
that are saturated with religious feeling.   The
legend of the Holy Grail and its influence on the
world during the Middle Ages ought to follow the
narrative of Christ.   The achievements of King
Arthur and his knights, and the life of Parsifal
should likewise be included in the program of this
period.   Parsifal is the same character as the Percival of Malory's "Le Morte d'Arthur," but the
mediæval bard Wolfram von Eschenbach, who, in
his "Knightly Song of Songs," gave to the world
the account from which the Parsifal tale is drawn,
was a master poet and man of much religious fire.
In his hands Parsifal became a distinct **and**

different character from the one Tennyson portrays in "Idylls of the King."

There should be used also stories of the martyrs of the early Christian Church, both among the Romans and in Europe during the Middle Ages. It was they who kept the flame of Christianity burning at such terrific cost—Wycliffe, Bernard of Menthon, Luther, and a host of others. The example of those to whom the Christian religion was so precious that they could endure hardship, persecution, and even die for it, carries a great lesson to the youth of to-day. As they follow the struggles of these heroes and realize something of the cost at which the faith of Christianity has been kept alive in the world, they come into a consciousness of the need that they themselves "carry on." They are like the inhabitants of a certain Greek city in their response to the appeal of one who stood ready to purchase with his sight, his limbs, or even his life, the welfare of his country, when he charged his fellow citizens to keep his laws, declaring, "Thou hast had Sparta allotted to thee. Adorn it!"

THOUGHT QUESTIONS

1. When should moral and religious education begin in order to be most effective? Why does religious instruction of little children sometimes meet with little success?

2. How is God most effectively introduced to the little child? Explain reason for answer.

3. Why should the same stories be retold often to little children? When should the retelling of a story cease?

4. How often should the same story be used in the entire program of religious education?
5. As a matter of classroom procedure, which should come first, the telling of the story or the discussion of the lesson? Why?
6. How can pictures be used to emphasize truths or help make the story vivid?
7. Why should the mother or teacher prepare the story from the Bible itself rather than from Bible storybooks?
8. Why should Bible reading and story-telling go hand in hand with older children?
9. Explain the use of stories as themes of pageantry, dramatization, essays, and debates.
10. Why is it necessary to proceed with great caution in using pageantry and dramatics in religious education work?

CHAPTER VII

THE TECHNIQUE OF STORY-TELLING

THERE are people who believe a course in story-telling is a waste of time, both for the student and the teacher. They maintain that if it is in one to tell stories one can do it, and if it is not, one cannot be taught.

It would be just as logical to argue that whoever has an aptitude for music or art will become a pianist or painter without instruction, and therefore it is a waste of time to take lessons. Yet any one who has watched the progress of an apt pupil under a good teacher knows what a mistaken idea that is.

A person may see a beautiful picture in his mind, but he cannot successfully paint that picture unless he knows how to mix pigments and apply them to canvas. He may have a vision of a splendid sculptured piece, but he will be unable to make that piece real without knowledge of how to shape marble, or to manipulate plaster into the caste preliminary to the completed statue. He must master the underlying principles of his art before he can become a successful creator. He can master them only when through instruction and long, laborious experiment and practice he has found out what they are.

There have been men who have won immortal

fame because of their achievements in the field of sculpture, painting, music, and literature. Unaided, they have risen to the heights of great achievement because of infinite capacity for work and painstaking attention to detail. But these have been individuals of supreme genius—Phidias, Michael Angelo, Tintoretto, Raphael, Leonardo da Vinci, Bach, Beethoven, Shakespeare, and a few others who have towered above their fellows as the Himalayas tower above the Indian plains. They were not average people, doing the work in the world of average, everyday men. Because of marvelous gifts they were able to work out for themselves, by the trial and error method, a mode of procedure that enabled them to achieve success. Michael Angelo could have in his mind an image of Moses or David, attack a block of marble with his chisel, and as if by miracle bring nobly executed figures from the rough slab. Nobody knows when or how he learned the art of sculpture. He simply carved, and carved gloriously.

But there are millions of people of average ability to one of flaming genius, and the ordinarily endowed individual must be taught. No matter in what field of art he chooses to work, he must learn the method of procedure from someone who has traveled the road he is endeavoring to travel. He must strive to make himself skillful in using the method which others have perfected.

Every person who loves the beautiful can achieve success in a small way in putting beauty into the world, provided he thinks he can, and is willing to exert himself in order to do it. He may not be able to draw, paint, or play a musical instrument with artistry that will bring him renown, but he will be able to give fuller expression to his own emotional life and help to enrich the lives of those in his immediate surroundings. The world needs every bit of ability that lies latent in human beings, and each individual should strive to develop his ability to the uttermost. It is a part of what he owes in service to mankind.

ALL PERSONS CAN LEARN TO TELL STORIES

Story-telling is an art in which it is possible for every person who is not handicapped by defects of speech to attain some degree of success. This art does not require special muscular control or acute sense of sound and color, as do most of the other arts. Whoever is intelligently interested in life can tell about the life he sees and knows. Whoever reads or hears a story sympathetically, has one of the essentials in depicting for others the happenings in that story. He may not do it skillfully, but he can let people know what he has seen and heard. If he masters the principles that govern story-telling, he can become skillful enough that his description will be pleasing to the hearer.

Technique of story-telling simple.—The technique of story-telling is neither complicated nor difficult of mastery. There are no fatiguing exercises to which hours upon hours of practice must be given—exercises that are of themselves without interest and are bearable only because they make the playing of a sonata or the singing of an aria possible later on. The practice necessary to enable one to succeed in the field of oral narration is pleasant practice, even while the mind is occupied with the mechanics of the art alone. The practice preliminary to the actual story-telling is not necessarily long. Once the principles are grasped a few hours of work will enable one to begin giving tales to an audience. Each time an inexperienced narrator entertains an audience he gains increased confidence and becomes more proficient in applying the principles.

Necessity of preparation and practice.—Although the course of preparation and practice for oral narration is neither laborious nor long, it is necessary that everyone who attempts to tell stories have this preparation. Without it he can no more succeed in holding an audience and in realizing his aim than a pianist can give delight if he begins a concert with stiffened and unskilled fingers, and without having previously interpreted to his own satisfaction each selection he attempts to interpret. The architect knows the laws of house-construction, but before directing men to begin the erection of a new edifice he definitely fits those laws to the piece of work that is to be done. He makes a detailed plan. He prepares in advance so that once the structure is begun he knows what the next step will be and why it is necessary in the building of that particular edifice. It is the same with the story-teller. He must plan each piece of work. Not only must he plan his work, but, by preparation and practice, he must train himself skillfully to carry out that plan.

PREPARING THE STORY

Success in story-telling is possible only when the spirit of the story fits into the teller's own mood. Upon first thought this seems difficult, but it really is not. Familiarity with situations and people makes us sympathetic toward them. The average stranger as we pass him in the street does not awaken our interest. Only as we see some one of a personality so striking that the dominant features of that personality are evident at first glance do we feel, "I'd like to know that person." But the average person, the one we pass without especially noticing, usually, proves to be interesting and appealing as we come to know his human qualities.

It is the same with stories. If it is a good tale, it contains a human appeal that cannot be resisted. Sometimes, in a first reading this appeal is missed because of the mood in which the reader happens to be, or because it is read carelessly and is not understood. But once the *heart* of the story is felt, once the characters are beheld as pulsing human beings, it arouses interest. There is awakened a desire to know what happens to them as they move through the tale. Therefore the narrator *must know each story*. He must know it in such a way that it will fit into his moods.

Knowing the story.—Knowing a story does not mean memorizing it word for word and sentence for sentence. It means having such a full knowledge of the chain of events that make up the sequence that they can be carried in the mind without effort. It means having a clear mental picture of every scene in which a portion of the action transpires. It means knowing the characters, their customs, impulses, and thoughts. It means *living with the story until it has become like a real experience to the teller*. Unless the tale is real to the narrator himself it will not become real to those who hear it. It cannot be an influence for quickened moral or religious feeling unless it seems an actual experience. Only as emotions are aroused in the hearer like those that incited to action the characters in the tale does the work of the narrator bear fruit. The child's nature will not be stirred deeply by a tale unless he has *felt* with the characters, unless he has *experienced* with them sorrow, pleasure, indignation, fear, contempt, pity, and various other feelings. Ideals are born and high purposes fostered only when the emotions have been touched.

Knowledge of story comes only through study.—Adequate knowledge of the setting, characters, and sequence of incidents in a tale comes only through careful study. To read a narrative once or twice is just the beginning of preparation. Ordinarily several readings are necessary to fix the order of events in the mind. Even if the mind is unusually retentive, one reading will not suffice to make the scenes vivid to the smallest detail, as they must be if the child is to live through them. Therefore the following course of preparation should be followed by the student ambitious to succeed as a narrator:

First, study the story to learn its plot.—The amount of time required for this will depend entirely upon the memory power of the student. Some, will have a clear grasp of the order of events after one reading; three or four readings will be necessary for others. But those to whom memorization is slow and tedious in the beginning will find the task less arduous as they work with stories. Each tale mastered makes the mastery of succeeding tales easier. It is not possible to develop a poor memory into a phenomenal one, but it is both possible and comparatively easy to improve it so that it will serve one without great labor.

Studying characters and setting.—After the plot has been mastered and the order of events fixed securely in the mind, the story should be studied again, this time with a view to the characters and setting. Now the student is concerned not so much with what the characters do as with why they act, the motive that lies behind their movements, and the outstanding character traits. In what kind of an environment do they live? Are their homes wretched hovels or homes in the full sense of the word?

An effort should be made to picture the country in which they work out their destinies. Is it plain or mountains, desert, well-tilled valley, or tangled jungle? If in town, is it picturesque or ugly? If a city, are the characters centered in a beautiful residence quarter or in a jostling, ill-smelling part where human beings are crowded together like cattle? The scenes and characters must be visualized. They must be seen and felt, as they are seen and felt in life. The narrator must react to them very much as he reacts to the people he meets, if through his portrayal the child is to react naturally and vitally to them. He must like and dislike them as he does in life. He must approve and disapprove their various acts as decisively as he approves and disapproves the conduct of his acquaintances.

Aids to visualization.—An excellent aid toward visualizing the characters and setting of a story is to portray them on paper. If the student is apt at drawing, much benefit will come through making pictures of the persons and scenes. Even if in the beginning these seem a trifle vague to him as he attempts to picture or represent them, they *will* take form.

This is what the illustrator does when commissioned to make pictures for a book or tale. He studies the story with a view to plot, characters, and setting. Especially is he concerned with the characters and the setting. He *lives* with the tale until these begin to be real to him. Then, as more and more clearly they work out in his mind, he gets them onto paper. Once having them in visible form they are *his* characters, and stay with him as a permanent possession.

Whether or not the student can illustrate his stories by drawings, he should use both characters and setting as themes of composition. Suppose one is preparing the narrative of the dream of Pharaoh and the interpretation by Joseph, as related in the forty-first chapter of Genesis, the following themes should be made the bases of drawings or composition:

The river scene in which the kine appear, Genesis 41. 1-4.

Scene in the palace when Pharaoh wakes from his dream, Genesis 41. 8-14.

The arraying and exalting of Joseph, Genesis 41. 39-45.

Scene of the famine in Egypt, Genesis 41. 54-57.

The meeting of Jacob and his sons on the return from Egypt, Genesis 42. 36-38.

Describing these scenes, either with words or the lines of a drawing, will make the story far more vivid. Before one can describe the various situations it is necessary to have definite, clear mental pictures of them. In thus working with the characters, the beginner in the field of oral narration will focus his attention upon them and will be able to recall them with greater ease.

To formulate written and oral descriptions of the characters aids greatly in securing the necessary vivid, complete conception that is so necessary. If it is not possible to give such descriptions, the student needs to put more study on the story. Until he can describe both persons and scenes in a tale he is not equipped for telling it. Joseph, Jacob, Reuben, Judah, and Israel should be described. How do they look? Is Joseph tall and of splendid bearing, or is he awkward and stocky? If the narrative gives a definite impression, there is a definite mental image of these men. If each does not stand out as a distinct character, the story should be read and reread until he does. The picture of Joseph in the narrator's mind may be very different from that portrayed by some of the painters of biblical scenes and characters. It may not even be correct from the standpoint of dress. But Joseph must be a *real person* to the story-teller or he will not be one to the child.

In recounting the tale the narrator will not describe each of these scenes and personages in detail; it is the impressions he has of them that are so important. In any field of teaching *it is necessary to know more than one makes use of.* Otherwise the child senses that something is lacking in the instructor. The master story-teller is richly steeped in his material. Hence he dispenses it with such

ease and spontaneity that he seems an unquench-
able fountain. The one of meager qualifications,
who knows but little more about his subject than
he is scheduled to teach, may be letter perfect in
such information as he possesses, yet intuitively
the child feels that the stream is about to run dry.
If the story-teller is to rise above mediocrity, he
must obtain an abundance of material. He must be
steeped in the imagery and feelings of his tale if it is
to be more than a dry chronicle to those who hear it.

How untrained story-tellers succeed.—There are
men and women, who, without formal training in
the technique of story-telling, can hold people
spellbound with their narration of the Bible tales.
A woman of meager schooling was the teacher of a
group of boys from nine to twelve, a lot of decidedly
rough fellows recruited from the worst district
of a large American manufacturing city. Yet she
held them with what seemed to be almost hypnotic
power as she told them the Old Testament stories.

Finally she moved away. A university girl, a
trained story-teller, took her place. The first
Sunday there were twenty-three boys present, the
usual number and the full enrollment of the class.
The following week nine came. A Sunday later
not one boy appeared. From the standpoint of
schooling there was no comparison between these
two teachers. The university girl had received her
bachelor's degree in English and was then doing
graduate work. She had had a course in story-
telling under an excellently qualified teacher. The
woman knew almost nothing of the literature of the
world. She had had no opportunity for such
study because the demands of her life made it

impossible for her to get to the public library, and there was no money with which to buy books of her own. But she knew her Bible. She had read and reread it—had absorbed all its color and romance. She had eagerly gleaned from sermons she had heard and from books borrowed from time to time, a vast amount of information concerning the ways of life in Bible lands and times. She was saturated with her subject and full of enthusiasm for it. Out of this rich store she gave freely to the boys in her care. She made the Hebrews appear as living, red-blooded people to them. Her knowledge of them was rich in detail. It was vividly interpreted, for she believed in them.

Writing the story preliminary to telling it.—Once the narrator is steeped in his story material, after he knows the plot and has visualized the characters in their various settings until he has clear mental pictures of them, it will be well for him to write out the tale as he would give it to an imaginary audience. There may not be time for this phase of preparation as a part of each lesson. The busy mother probably cannot do it at all. But the student who is fitting himself for the great work of religious education should write out his stories whenever possible. This test will prove to him whether or not he is ready to tell them. If he cannot make a written version with ease, he needs more study. Until he can put a narrative upon paper without hesitation he will not be able to tell it without hesitation. It is not yet his story so that he can make it seem valuable to the children.

Describing the scenes of the tale versus remembering the words.—Finally, when the student is ready to tell the story, he should practice it. He should deliver it to an imaginary audience, always with his attention upon the scenes and characters. If he has lived with the tale until it seems like a part of his own experience, the words with which to describe those scenes will come, just as words come to a sailor when he recounts his experiences at sea, because he knows what he is talking about. A person may have no language gift, and be slow of speech in regard to most subjects, but when he tells of something through which he has lived, he does not fail to interest those who hear.

This point can hardly be emphasized too strongly. *Always attention should be centered on the scenes and characters of a story.* The thought should be of the pictures and activities that constitute the plot, and words with which to describe those activities and pictures will not fail one. If, on the other hand, the mind is centered on trying to remember the book version of the narrative, if a word or sentence cannot be recalled when needed, failure is sure to result. In thinking about the language, vivid mental pictures are impossible. There does not exist any well-stocked supply house of imagery from which the narrator who is thinking about words can draw.

Repeating words of book version is not story-telling.—There are many stories in portions of which the language is so exquisite that to change it in any way is to have the children lose much. Such portions should be memorized and given as in the book version. These may be bits of dialogue, an exceptionally gripping opening paragraph, climax or ending containing a sentence that should be left with the child. When these memorized portions are given, the narrator should throw his whole effort into giving them to the full possibility of their dramatic effect. But to attempt to learn a story from beginning to end, and to give it exactly as it is told in the book, is bad story-telling procedure. In fact, it is not story-telling at all. It is a recitation, or dramatic reading.

A child will not react to even the best of dramatic reading as he reacts to the moderately well-told tale. The former makes the situations and characters seem less real to him. He senses that something has been learned. It is not spontaneous and natural, like the outpouring of an experience. It is formal. One of the chief charms of story-telling to a child is its informality. He feels a sense of intimacy with the characters in a tale that is well told. He does not feel this intimacy with the characters in a recitation.

Dramatic reading and story-telling are two distinct arts. Each has its place in the culture program of present-day life, but the place of dramatic reading in the program of child education is in supplementing story-telling. It may be used to excellent advantage to help emphasize a story that has been told. For instance, if the account of the Exodus is given to boys and girls in the adventure period, with emphasis upon Moses the leader, the reading of Alexander's "Burial of Moses" will be a valuable finale to the tale. It will give to the class a vivid and lasting impression of the close of the earthly career of the great lawgiver of the Hebrews. But never should such reading or recitation supplant telling the story.

Telling the Story

When the tale has been thoroughly prepared as it should be, the narrator can face his hearers equipped for real accomplishment. He can lead them into the region where the action of the story transpires. He is not groping for words, or trying to remember what happens next. He is recounting experiences through which the characters have lived, and through which he has lived with them. He is not giving a record of these experiences through laborious effort. He is recounting them with spontaneity and buoyant feeling, as he describes a happening in his life. Because of this buoyant feeling he can make the message of the story clear and vital to his auditors as he cannot do if his mind is concentrated upon the language and the order of events. He can tell the story with an enthusiasm and earnestness that will stir productive feeling, that will create ideals and high purpose and result in worthy action.

Look into the eyes of the auditors.—The story-teller should be direct and forceful in his manner. His glance should travel along the faces of his hearers. It should not be upon the floor or ceiling, or rambling along the windows. He should look into the eyes of those who make up his audience. He is talking to them. He should by his manner make them feel that he is confiding something to them, that he is revealing to them some rare experience or bit of knowledge. They will not have this feeling of participating with him if he stares into space.

Make the vocabulary fit the story.—It is of great importance that the language in which a tale is told should fit the spirit of that tale. An account of a runaway horse should be described in terse, short sentences, and, for the most part, short words. Do not say, "The animal saw the locomotive, gave a momentary start of alarm, went galloping down the street." Say instead, "The spirited creature heard the whistle of the engine. He saw the great black object moving toward him, closer, closer, shrieking as it came. His eyes rolled with terror. He snorted, pawing around the post where he was tied. Then, with a mighty lunge, he broke the rope that held him and tore madly down the street."

A description of a desert, or slow-moving river, each of which is suggestive of repose, would go something like this: "The desert shimmered under the noonday sun, tawny, like the pelt of a lion, stretching away to the purple mountains piled along the Arizona border." "The river moved slowly, like some sluggish living thing, across the undulating plain country, and into the yucca thicket that fringed the coast."

Children instinctively feel whether or not the language in which a story is told is suitable to the characters and actions of that story. In that popular nursery tale, "The Three Billy Goats," the pleasure of the little people hearing it is very keen if one says, "Trip-trap, trip-trap, trip-trap, Big Billy Goat Gruff went over the bridge." It is not nearly so enjoyable to them if one says merely, "Big Billy Goat Gruff went over the bridge."

Vocabulary and sentence structure that *fit* the scenes and action of the tale—this is a cardinal point for the narrator to remember.

Dialogue.—Talking characters help to make the story vivid. John said to his mother, "I give you my word of honor to be home by six," is more dramatic than "John promised his mother to be home by six o'clock." This is especially true if the voice of the narrator simulates the voices of the characters, the gruff speech of the crabbed old man, the gentle tones of the good princess, and the drawling ones of lazy Peter. An oral story cannot be made up wholly of dialogue. But dialogue interspersed with bits of narrative heightens dramatic effect. And dialogue should be realistic. It should be true in tone to the character. Moreover, it should be given in the vocabulary the character would be *likely* to use.

Change in rate of speaking.—Another thing that helps to make a tale dramatic to those who hear it is to vary the rate of the telling to fit the action. Where the deer breaks into the garden and goes crashing among the shrubbery the movement speeds. Where there is a description of the weary princess drowsing in the sunlight, the rate of movement is slow. Judgment and ingenuity on the part of the narrator must mark the telling of each story. Dialogue and varied movement both, must be skillfully used to heighten dramatic effect.

The pause in story-telling.—One of the greatest aids of all in making a tale dramatic to the hearers is to use the pause. Pause is the highest form of emphasis in oral delivery, and intensifies eagerness to know what is about to happen. "John saw the snarling dog lunge toward him, and then—" Instantly the children are tense with eagerness to know what comes next. They imagine and wonder.

Pause is also the most effective means of reviving interest that has begun to wane. When John shows by his face and manner that his mind is wandering from the thread of the tale say, "And John, the very next minute—" Quickly he is recalled to the scene of the tale. He wonders what happened the next minute.

Pause is also an aid to the narrator who has the misfortune to lose her audience because of having poorly prepared the tale. It serves the double purpose of enabling her to think of what to do or say *next* at the same time that she regains attention.

Action and gesture in story-telling.—When telling a story the main thing to remember is that the work of the narrator is to describe scenes and actions. He should *tell* what the characters do as they move through the tale, but he should *not represent* their actions. He should not jump, bend, distort his body and attempt to imitate the characters. Action on the part of the story-teller attracts attention to himself, which is a distinct weakness. His business is to focus the interest of his hearers upon the scenes in the tale. To introduce movements of the body into the narrative or indulge in facial gymnastics, leads the mind of the auditor away from the tale to the teller. He should keep himself in the background. Not he but the characters in the narrative hold the center of the stage. When the children are thinking about how funny the story-teller looks they are not thinking about the story. They may be entertained by his antics, but are not catching the spirit and message of the tale.

This answers the question of gesture. It does not mean, however, that the narrator must be motionless as a wooden image. Gesture should be used if it comes naturally. But all violent body and facial movements are to be avoided. There should be no jumping, twisting, no body poses of any kind. If one gesticulates naturally in talking, if gesture accompanies the ordinary conversation, it is not objectionable in the story-teller. Under such conditions it is transformed in the narrative and seems part of it. But never should it be introduced for studied effect. The great underlying principle of oral narration is that it must be natural. A story that abounds in gesture introduced for effect is not natural. Therefore, from an artistic standpoint it is bad.

The voice should be natural.—The voice of the narrator should be that used in his natural speaking. He should not attempt tone effects any more than he should attempt those of posture. In dialogue portions that simulate as nearly as possible the voices of the characters increase the vividness to the child. But in the narrative parts the voice should be that of the story-teller's everyday speech. Voice is a medium through which the hearers see the people and scenes in a tale. It should be used in a manner so natural, so much a part of the one who gives the story, that there will be no thought in the minds of the auditors of how his tones sound.

All this sums up in the statement that the narrator who has lived with the story until it is like a personal experience will not become affected or commit faults of either tone or gesture. The true story-teller will not be able to take himself away from the scene of the tale sufficiently to think about how to pitch his voice at this point or hold his body at that. He will be living the story, and the children

will live it with him. Under such conditions the
lessons that come to them will not be forgotten.

Do not moralize in telling a story.—There is one
vital principle the narrator must make his own
if he is to realize his aim. He should not moralize.
He should not tell what he thinks about the behavior
of Esau when he sells his birthright, of Eve when she
heeds the voice of the serpent, or of any other
character in any tale. He must take his hearers
to the scene of the story and let them *see for themselves and draw their own conclusions*. To point a
moral while giving a narrative is the worst kind of
pedagogy and art. The child sees the moral for
himself if the tale is skillfully presented. He resents
having the story-teller stop and call attention to
what is already clear, because it breaks the thread
of the tale and spoils his pleasure in it. He wants
to know what happens next, not what the story-
teller thinks about what has happened.

The moral of the tale may be considered after it is
finished, when it is beneficial to have some discussion regarding it. But this discussion must be
skillfully handled if it is to be of real value. The
child should not get the idea that the story was
told just to teach him something. He does not
want to be taught. Teaching is most effectively
accomplished by one who entertains children, who
leads them to see for themselves the consequence
of right or wrong conduct, who is the medium
through which unconsciously they absorb lessons
they should learn.

The story-teller then, should aim to lead his
hearers into regions where they will have the experiences which he wishes them to have. In order

to do this he must wipe out all consciousness of self, and he can accomplish this only by so completely losing himself in the events and characters that he forgets that he, as an individual, exists. Then will he become to his hearers a magician who spirits them into a fascinating, distant realm. Then, and then only, through living, vivid experience, will he succeed in creating moods out of which ideals and faith are born.

Thought Questions

1. Why are story-telling courses helpful even to those with special aptitude for telling stories?
2. Explain the steps in preparing a story for telling.
3. Name two aids to visualization, and explain why each is helpful.
4. What is the secret of the success of some untrained story-tellers?
5. Why is it bad story-telling procedure to memorize the book version of a story?
6. What is the difference between story-telling and dramatic reading?
7. What is meant by making the vocabulary fit a story?
8. Why is it advisable to use dialogue in story-telling? to change the rate of speaking? Explain the value of pause in story-telling.
9. Should action and gesture be used in telling a story? Explain answer. What voice should be employed in telling a story?

CHAPTER VIII

TYPES OF STORIES AND THEIR USES

A WIDE variety of types of stories is found in the literature of the world, and each type has fulfilled some definite purpose in transmitting the feeling, thought, and history of the race. There are epic stories and historical romance. There is myth, fairy tale, legend, realistic story, parable, and fable. There are tales of adventure, love stories, and allegorical narratives. Each type has grown somewhere and at some time out of the life of a people. The essential nature of each determines the particular use to which it can be put in the program of religious education.

CHARACTERISTICS OF THE DIFFERENT TYPES

These stories represent man's inner struggles and desires. They portray not only what he actually has done in working out his destiny, but what he has eagerly yearned to do. They mirror life or some phase of life. No tale that has lived was written originally for the purpose of winning fame or making money for its author. It is the outpouring of its writer's soul, or of the souls of others whose workings have been revealed to him. Although often both fame and money have come of the writing, the urge that prompted it was something deeper and more vital than eagerness to attract the public eye. It was a vent for pent-up feeling as necessary to one who has observed broadly and thought deeply as a steam valve is to an engine. That is why whoever works in the field of literature, either as a writer or as an oral narrator, should approach his work with reverence and something of humility. In giving stories he is drawing back the veil from the most intimate and sacred phases of the experiences of those who have wrought nobly.

Fairy tales.—As already stated, the fairy tales that have come down the centuries were religious stories in the beginning. They have undergone many transitions in their journey through the ages. They have become modified to fit conditions of life in which those among whom we find them lived. In the beginning they were colored by the character of the country in which they were formed, those that originated in lands of ice-bound, storm-racked winters, wild mountains, deep ravines, far-reaching, austere deserts and wind-whipped steppes being made up of fiercer personages than the ones found in tales that grew in countries where the landscape was one of mild beauty and the climate balmy and gentle. The giants of the former are repulsive and cruel, and even the fairy god-mothers are severe. The men and women in the tales of rugged lands are stronger, and the children are sturdier than those in regions where the physical features are less wild.

Likewise, as people moved from one land to another, the characters in their stories grew fiercer or gentler, according to the scenery of the new location. In Scandinavia, where the mountains are rugged, the coasts jagged and dangerous, and the cataracts voluminous and raging, and in Finland, Iceland, and Russia, where men are icebound for many months and where blizzards and windstorms rage through the mountains and sweep vast plains, the struggle for existence is bitter, and there the tales are like the country—stern and austere. They typify the savage nature that encompasses the people among whom they grew. But in Belgium, Germany, Italy, and France, where the face of nature is milder, a gentler lot of supernatural creatures are heroes of the stories. The kobolds of Danish fireside tales are a more affable lot of little people than the trolls of the northernmost fjords. Gentler too are the brownies of Scotland and the leprechauns of Ireland, where the ocean is not as savage as under the midnight sun, where there is not the terrific depth of ravine or height of mountain that we find in Norway.

The little people of the Austrian and German mountains, the nixies, who figure in the stories of the Thuringian and Bavarian peasants, are winsome whether they are doers of evil or good, and sometimes among them we find both. The fées of France are lovable, gracious folk, the embodiment of beauty and charm. The bad fairies in the French peasant narratives are less repulsive than those in lands further north.

The person who reads translated fairy stories gets a poor idea of the characteristics of the tales of different lands, because most books of such narratives as we have them in the United States and England are a heterogeneous collection of stories from a dozen different countries. All of the spritelike creatures are called fairies, and the grotesque little fellows are brownies, gnomes, or dwarfs.

He who reads these volumes does not make the acquaintance of the kobolds of the Danish glens, the nixies of the German highlands, Rübezahl and the merry little people of the Bohemian mountains and the rest of the interesting company of supernatural folk that troop through the racial tales. But the folk-lorist, who makes his collection at the firesides of the peasants and hears the stories told in their tongue, learns that those of different lands are as distinctive from each other as the cultured resident of a city is from the gipsies of the plains.

In the Maritime Alps, back of the French Riviera, many of the peasant tales cluster around Esterella, a nymph who entices men from their homes. But she does not send them to destruction. She leads them forever in pursuit of her over the crags and cliffs, but does not cause death. But some five hundred miles north of the Riviera, where the Rhine gorge is steep and fissured and the winters are fierce compared with those of the south, is the river maiden called Lorelei, whose delight is to lure sailors to their doom in the whirlpool at the foot of the cliffs. She is a harder, more northern character than Esterella, as in turn the Witch Woman of the Trolltinder, the mountain country of Scandinavia believed to be haunted by supernatural folk, is harder than the Lorelei.

Two interesting exceptions to the prevailing softness of fairy-folk among the tales of France are those of Brittany, and the mountain country of Auvergne. Beside the savage ocean that lashes the Breton coast in the region of Cape Finisterr, life has been a bitter struggle for the peasants, a never-ending battle against the elements. Around the firesides of Brittany the folk-lorist finds stories more rugged than he finds in the interior of the land or on the shore of the Mediterranean. Beautiful fairies and high-souled kings move through the narratives, but they dispense justice with a less merciful hand than do those of the south. The giants in the tales of Brittany are more repulsive and terrible than those met on the Loire and Rhone.

It is the same among the mountains of Auvergne, the ancient volcanic region where the ways of men are more primitive than in any other part of France and where the landscape is austere. Here, where great, half-obliterated ropes of lava are heaped along the slopes like masses of dead serpents, there is little that is graceful or mild about the face of nature. Austerity and bareness reign. In this section we find stories so fierce in their characters that they seem not to belong to France at all. They are more like those of Russia and Scandinavia, the most savage of all European narratives.

One might go on through many pages citing examples to show how truthfully racial tales reflect the atmosphere and natural features of lands in which they grew. Not only fairy tales, but myths, epics, and legends have undergone changes to fit changed conditions of life. Siguard, the Volsung of the Norwegian sagas, and Siegfried, of the German Nibelungenlied, are the same character. The stories have come from the same ancient source. Gentleness is not the salient characteristic of Siegfried, but he is hardly as fierce a personage as Sigurd, his northern counterpart. In some way, during very remote times, the nucleus of the Sigurd tale was carried to Germanic regions by tribes wandering southward. There, as centuries passed, it changed to fit the lives of people among less savage surroundings until it became another story, with fewer harsh angles and ruthless deeds.

The statement is sometimes made that the fairy tales of some lands are more cruel in character than those of others because the people are more cruel by nature. From the standpoint of the folk-lorist this statement needs to be qualified. Racial tales, and by this is meant all stories that have come down the centuries and that abound in supernatural happenings, reflect the *conditions in which the men lived among whom they originated*. The struggle and desire to overcome that which is terrifying and hard in life results in acquired traits that are hardy. The giants and fairies, as well as the human folk of these narratives, are fierce and cruel or kindly and gentle because they symbolize not original human nature, but human nature as modified by the country of those to whom the tales were both science and religion.

The cruel story of Bluebeard does not contradict this principle. First of all, Bluebeard is not a pure French fairy tale. It is a corrupted legend dating from the early Middle Ages, that recounts the bloody procedure of a lord of northern France. To rank it with fairy tales is as incorrect as to place in this list such modern fanciful yarns as "The Wizard of Oz" or "The Adventures of Dr. Doolittle." Secondly, it is not fair to judge the folk-lore of any country by one, or even by half a dozen tales. Only by becoming familiar with the history of a story or group of stories, the nature of the region from which it sprang, and the conditions under which the people lived, is one qualified to say what it symbolizes.

The origin and nature of myths.—Myth, like fairy tale, is the expression of primitive man's religion. Fairy tales are largely made up of remnants of primitive nature-myth. There are nature- and animal-myths dating from very remote times that tell how the fox got its fur, the leopard its spots, and the cause of summer and winter, according to early man's ideas. But myth as we think of it among the peoples of Europe, is of later origin than fairy tales and primitive nature-myth. It grew out of the life of the people after they had come to have definite ideas concerning religious things and the forces of nature. When myth evolved man had a fixed religious belief. When fairy tales were formed he was groping, wondering, and fearful. All was unknown. His stories portray what he vaguely imagined Omnipotence might be and what he desired it to be. In myth he was beginning to find his place in the universe and to have convictions as to the meaning of that universe.

History and historical romance.—History is an account of what has actually happened, a record of events gone by. Historical romance is partly history and partly fiction. It is a recounting of something that really has happened, but into it are introduced imaginary incidents or characters. Sometimes too even the facts of historical romance are set in a fanciful background. Some of the characters that move through it have actually lived, but with them are associated others that are the creation of the author. Both in characters and setting, historical romance is a blending of the real and the imaginary. It rests on a foundation of truth, but many of the blocks of the structure are composed of fiction.

Legend.—Legend is a form of narrative the facts of which are believed to be true by those among whom it is found, and in the main its events have happened. But some of them cannot be verified by historical record, although by those who gave them to the next generation they were believed to have occurred. Legends contain some supernatural element, a miracle, vision or marvelous happening. They are wonder tales that rest on a barely discoverable foundation of truth. The King Arthur of history was a crude British chieftain of the sixth century. There is no historic record of the many deeds attributed to him and his knights in the Arthurian cycle of romances. He was a warrior who fought numerous battles. Judged by the standards of his day he was a valiant and upright man. As stories of his achievements went down the generations they were exaggerated, as is likely to happen when tales pass through many mouths, even though there is no intent to deceive. Consequently, as the homage of the tellers dwelt upon these exaggerated exploits, with the passing of a century or two he became a demigod—a man of miraculous power. Throughout the closing years of the Dark Ages and during mediæval times these legends of King Arthur and his knights were believed as implicitly as ever history was believed. Yet none of the achievements of Percival, Launcelot or their associates can be verified by the chronicles of the time in which they are supposed to have occurred.

Allegory, parable and fable.—In allegory, virtues

and vices, characteristics, moods, nations, cities, the seasons, etc., are personified and represented as human beings. Truth, deceit, greed, humility, avarice, peace, and war, work out their problems as persons. By their deeds and words lessons are taught. During the Dark and Middle Ages allegory was a favorite form of narrative with religious workers, and was used to show the triumph of faith over heresy, of goodness over sin. Allegory is still much employed in religious and moral education, especially in the Catholic Church. It is used particularly in pageantry where the triumph of community spirit and progress is shown. But it is not a popular type of story with boys and girls below the adolescent period. Unless it is handled in a masterly way the moral is too obvious, and children do not take kindly to the idea of undisguised moralizing. The idealism of allegory makes it appealing to older young people. It is therefore often used to advantage with those in adolescent years. But, generally speaking, it is of little value to younger folk. A nearly adult intelligence is necessary to grasp its symbolism. Those below the age of fourteen and fifteen are usually unequal to the task.

Parable, like allegory, is intended to point to a moral or to teach a lesson. But parable differs from allegory in this respect: into allegory impossible characters and situations are introduced. In parable the characters are human beings and the events are such as actually occur. Christ, in his teaching used the parable freely, and the best idea of what this form of narrative is will be obtained by reading the parables of the New Testament.

Fable, in its elements, is like parable. It is intended to teach a lesson, but its happenings take place among animals or inanimate things, stones, trees, the wind and sun, etc. The best examples of fables to which most readers have access are those of Æsop, although thousands of even more ancient origin are found floating through the folklore of the world. Those of Æsop are partly folktale and partly creations of his own, like the stories of Hans Christian Andersen. In many of them there is a skillful blending of ancient fireside tales and his own imagination. The fables of La Fontaine are almost entirely bits of folk-lore gathered from French peasants and retold in verse. Fable is a very pleasing from of narrative to little children, because, according to their ideas, all the events in it happened in the long ago.

Epic.—Epic is made up of stories that have lived through generations as myths or legends, and have then been worked into a consecutive chain so as to form the plot of a great story. All of the achievements or events in an epic center around some national hero like Charlemagne, Roland, Ogier the Dane, or King Arthur. Moreover, epics are in poetic form. For century after century the scattered tales that comprise them had been told and retold in camps and around firesides. Finally some bard or minstrel worked them into a connected plot and put them into blank verse or rime. Thus they have come down to us.

An epic represents the slow gathering of a large number of myths, legends, and folk-tales by people of succeeding generations. It is grouped around some national hero. For instance, scattered tales of achievements of supermen, that in the beginning symbolized the sun and the various forces of nature and were an expression of religious belief, gradually came to be centered around King Arthur, Pwyll, hero of the Mabinogian, Charlemagne, Roland or Ogier the Dane. Then a great poet worked them into artistic form and gave them to the world as a completed drama. As one folklorist says, epic is the work of personality playing upon broad culture material.

In Greece it was Homer who took the tales of his people in their fragmentary form and made them into the *Iliad* and the *Odyssey*. In France, under the genius of Thomas Malory, ancient recitals of deeds of the Round Table brotherhood became Le Morte d'Arthur. Almost two hundred years before the time of Malory, Walther von der Vogelweide did the same thing in Germany. Under the play of his imagination these same scattered legends of men seeking the Holy Grail became the noble epic that during the Middle Ages bore the name of "The Knightly Song of Songs," and that the world now reveres as the story of "Parsifal." Nobody knows who it was who fashioned the life of the Cid Campeador into the Spanish epic poem that bears his name, or who shaped the tales of northern and central Europe and the British Isles into Beowulf, the Volsunga Saga, the Nibelungenlied, the Kalevala and the Mabinogian. But the history of their development is the same as that of the others. First, they were scattered bits of narrative sung and recounted by the people. Then some poet visioned them as a connected drama and gave them to the world as such.

EDUCATIONAL USES OF THE VARIOUS TYPES

Thus it will be seen that fairy tale, myth, legend, fable, parable, epic, allegory, historical romance, and history are very ancient types of tales. They represent the thought and spiritual growth of the race during its early stages, as well as its actual achievements. The developing child needs each of these types of tales somewhere in his course from birth to maturity. Roughly speaking, primitive nature myth and animal stories arouse his interest during the first five or six years of his life, because then his curiosity concerning animals is running high, and because in that stage of his life all things are possible to him.

Fairy tales feed during the period of fancy that follows the baby days, the time between the ages of five or six and nine or ten. Epic and adventure stories satisfy when the boy or girl is in fancy a young hero or heroine in paths of mighty achievement. Much of history and historical romance is also enjoyed in this adventure period.

Epic, history, and historical romance are also food for young people in the adolescent period, according to the emphasis they place upon pure adventure or achievement of high idealism, and how they deal with the two sexes. This also is the time when allegory means most.

Myth, unless its events are such that it makes an adventure story, or one that is a prototype of a fairy tale, and therefore of interest to younger children, belongs in the romantic period or age of adolescence. At this time, understanding of the religious striving of men has sufficiently developed in boys and girls for them to accept with sympathy what expresses the early man's religious aspirations. Even if scattered myths of Greece and other nations, *as hero stories* or fairy tales, have been given during an earlier age, myth *as the religion* of the Greeks, Romans, and Scandinavians belongs in the romantic, or adolescent period.

Legend, like history and historical romance, is most appealing in the heroic and in the romantic periods, according to the nature of its happenings. In all this discussion of the suitability of materials to meet the needs of the various age levels, provision must be made for wide variations due to the influence of environment.

Every type of tale found in the Bible.—Every type of narrative is to be found in the Bible. There are wonder stories illustrating lessons of the Hebrew narrators and recounting achievements that have all the moving appeal of fairy tales to the young child. There is the counterpart of myth, of fable, of legend, of epic, of historical romance, and there is history itself. There is allegory and parable. There is adventure as rich in happening as any the world has yet heard.

The life of Abraham, Isaac, Jacob, Joseph, Moses, Joshua, David, and Solomon each makes an epic. So also does the life of Christ. The Bible is a glorious repository of epics, and, therefore, if presented as a series of mighty dramas centering around the life of one of the outstanding heroes, it is the Book of books for boys and girls in both the adventure and adolescent periods, as great in interest and story appeal to them as in ethical and spiritual value.

It should be the aim of whoever works with youth in these two periods to give them the great epics of the Old and New Testaments. They have had many of the scattered stories during the earlier periods, just as the race had fragmentary tales of the various heroes before it received them in epic form. Following those periods they should be given as a connected drama, that young people may behold as great personages the heroes around whom the fragments center, and in realizing the splendor and worth of these heroes, feel a desire to emulate them.

In fact, if one knows the Bible well enough, it is possible from it alone to satisfy every story need of the child from infancy to manhood. But this can be done only by those to whom the life and thought of the Hebrews is as familiar as the narratives themselves. Otherwise they cannot be given against the rich background that makes them satisfying and complete.

Analyzing a story to determine its place in the educational program.—Because of lack of knowledge of the Bible and Bible times and customs, many workers in the religious field need to glean much material from other sources, in order that the children under their care may be nourished to the uttermost. As has been stated elsewhere, in making up a program of narratives outside the Scriptures, it is advisable to keep largely to the old tales, those that have stood the test of time. But among modern stories there are many valuable ones to use in the spiritual guidance of the child. In order to separate the chaff from the wheat in this material of later origin it is necessary to know how to analyze a story, both as to structure, content, and suitability for children in the various stages of development. It should be tested according to the following standards:

Structure.—To determine whether or not a tale is suitable for oral telling.

Has it a clearly defined plot?

Do the events follow each other in a logical sequence?

Does each incident carry over and add something to the action of the succeeding one?

Is each incident *necessary* to the unwinding of the thread of the story?

If not, which ones can be eliminated?

Does the plot hold interest from beginning to end?

Does interest steadily and rapidly increase and culminate in a gripping climax?

After the climax is reached are the characters ushered off the stage without delay, naturally but not too abruptly?

Are the characters sufficiently lifelike that one becomes sympathetic toward them?

Content.—Does the story carry a message without being preachy?

Does it pulse with religious feeling?

Does it ring true?

Age Suitability.—What type of tale is it, realistic or fanciful?

If realistic, will its appeal be to little children, those in the first period of realism, or to boys and girls of the adventure craving years?

If fanciful, will it satisfy children who crave wonder stories and fairy tales, or those in the romantic period, or age of adolescence?

If, when measured by the structure test, the tale is found to be suitable for telling, or can be made suitable by the elimination of extraneous matter, if it carries a worth-while message and tends to arouse religious feeling, the narrator may safely include it in his program, provided its appeal is to children of the age he teaches. The test of age suitability decides that. If it is not suited to those of adolescent years, he who guides boys and girls in the adventure period should not use it. These younger folk may follow it with moderate interest, but it should not be given to them, because there are other narratives that will serve them better. It is not fair to give food which children have outgrown, or that which they only partially digest, when in the great world of stories there is sufficient material to nourish them to the uttermost throughout each stage of their development.

THOUGHT QUESTIONS

1. Describe what fairy tales are and what they have meant in the life of the race?
2. What are myths, and how did they originate?
3. Define legend, allegory, parable, and fable and tell where each can be used with value in religious education?
4. Describe the development of epic, and its place in the education of the child.
5. What types of stories de we find in the Bible?
6. Explain how a story should be analyzed to determine its place in the educational program.

CHAPTER IX

SOURCES OF STORY MATERIAL

MUCH supplementary material of great value in religious training is to be found outside the Bible. Some of this material helps to emphasize the principles and truths that the Bible stories demonstrate. Moreover, if the biblical characters are to be presented in a setting that makes them vivid and gripping, the person who tells the stories must be saturated with the color and atmosphere of the Bible. The teacher in the religious field needs to know much about the sources of material from which he can draw with benefit in his work, and to use this material freely. It should be his constant aim to learn all he can learn that will tend to make the people of the Old and New Testaments real human beings to him. They must be real to him before he can make them real to the children. Unless they are real to the children the lessons their lives teach will not be clearly understood or deeply impressed. The characters can be real to the narrator only when he beholds them in the environment in which they worked out their destinies.

MATERIAL TENDING TO EMPHASIZE THE COLOR AND ATMOSPHERE OF THE BIBLE

No matter what the age of the children with whom he works, the person who tells stories for the pur-

pose of instilling religious ideals and strengthening
religious faith needs to know something of the Holy
Land, its various peoples, geography, and customs.
Without this knowledge he can no more give a vivid
impression of the characters who move through the
tales than the writer who knows nothing of the
range country can make a cowboy story ring with
spontaneity and conviction. The teacher of young
children and the teacher of adolescents each
pictures personages who lived in Israel during
Bible times. Therefore he needs to know about
the country and the people in the period of which
he tells.

Geography of the Holy Land.—Familiarity with
the geography of the Holy Land does not mean
that one should know all the details of lowland and
hill country. Because of the amount of time
required for gaining such information it is almost
out of the question for the average worker to amass
such a fund of knowledge, nor is it necessary that
he should have it. But the highlights of the geography of the Bible country should be very clear to
him. He should see Palestine as it lay in the sunlight of Old Testament times, on one of the main
travel routes of the ancient world. He should be
able to glimpse its position between Egypt on the
south and Mesopotamia on the north, and connected with those lands by caravan lines that were
the great highways of antiquity. When a story
of the Philistines is told there should be in the mind
of the teller a picture of the fertile coastal plain in
which the cities of these tribes stood. There should
be an understanding of the location of Tyre and
Sidon, Babylonia, Samaria, the land of Shinar,

Beersheba, Bethlehem, Mount Sinai, and the valleys, mountains, and deserts among which the life of Israel pulsed. A map will give the location of the places but it will not give the color and atmosphere that make Palestine a real country. Some historical or human geography of this region should be studied. Some book in which the points of interest are not merely located on a chart, but are shown as the scenes of stories that have been enacted there. Any of the following works will be excellent for this purpose.

A Historic Geography of the Holy Land—Smith (Doran).

Biblical Geography and History—Kent.

The Geography of Bible Lands—Rena L. Crosby.

The Land of Israel—Stewart.

Historic Geography of Bible Lands—Calkins.

Hilltops in Galilee—Harold Speakman.

The first-named of the above books is the more comprehensive, and to the student who has the time for detailed study it will be invaluable. Those who prefer a briefer work will find any of the others very helpful.

The last-named work is not a historical geography, but it is rich in pictures of Palestine, both during biblical times and to-day and will greatly aid the story-telling in visualizing the country.

Customs.—Beside a knowledge of the geography of Palestine, the story-teller in the religious field needs to know something of the customs and ways of life in Bible lands and times—how the people dressed, the food they ate, the industries they followed, and the organization of their family life. When he speaks of Pharisees, Sadducees, scribes, or **Levites,** he should know the place of those men in the social order of their day. He should have a comprehension of the festivals and religious observances of the ancient Hebrews, and some understanding of their laws.

Life and Literature of the Ancient Hebrews, by Lyman Abbott, is a graphic detailed exposition of the manners and customs of those days. *Hebrew Life and Thought* by Louise Seymour Houghton (University of Chicago Press), covers the same field in an equally comprehensive manner. Other books dealing with the manners, customs and ways of life of the Israelites are the following:

Bible Manners and Customs—Mackie.

Jewish Artisan Life in the Time of Jesus—Delitzsch.

Jewish Social Life—Edersheim.

Hebrew Life and Times—Hunting.

Tales and Customs of the Ancient Hebrews—Herbst.

Retold Bible Stories.—Some religious leaders maintain that whatever the teacher cannot himself get from the Bible is not worth his telling to children. This does not mean that the material is not worth telling, but that anything the narrator cannot himself glean from the book of books will be of little value to those to whom he gives it. Unless he himself can draw it from the Bible he cannot make it real to his hearers. It cannot be successfully challenged that the storybook of whoever undertakes to guide the child's spiritual training should be the Bible itself. But the stories should not be prepared entirely from the retold narratives as given in the lesson leaflets. For the heart and substance of the tale, one should go to the fountain-head, to the two Testaments, which are a never-failing source of food and inspiration. This rule should be the guiding one for the mother or teacher. The story as given in the Bible should be read until it is very vivid, until the teller is saturated with both its spirit and language. Then he will have a standard by which to judge of the usefulness of supplementary materials as well as of lesson-leaf versions.

Because the tales in the lesson leaflets, and in some of the Bible storybooks, are prepared by experts, they are very helpful, and should not be neglected. They should be read and studied along with the Bible itself. From this reading and study, bits of color and atmosphere are sometimes gained that otherwise might be missed. It is a good thing to see scenes and events as others have seen them, and to compare or contrast those impressions with our own. Many shades of green make up the carpet of forest and grass that covers a hillside, yet in seeing the blend of color the untrained observer may have an imperfect idea of the numerous tints that comprise the whole. Likewise, a person may miss in a word-picture details that another sees. Therefore, the religious worker should read as many good Bible story-books as possible. All of the following are excellent works:

Old, Old Tales from the Old, Old Book.—Smith.

A Child's Life of Christ—Dearmer.

A Child's Guide to the Bible—Hodges.

Stories from the Best of Books—Sangster and Yonge.

Bible Stories to Read and Tell—Olcott.

Christ Child Tales—Proudfoot.

The Illustrated Bible Story Book—Loveland.

Non-biblical Material

There is a wealth of material outside the Bible that will greatly enrich the child's spiritual life. Some of the more important types are: nature material, national and religious epics, and historical—especially biographical materials.

In the child's thinking God is naturally identified with nature. Therefore religious feeling and faith may be aroused in him by stories of plant and animal life, of stars and rainbow, of winds, frost, sunshine, and changing seasons. Especially is this true of the little child, who feels himself akin to the animal and plant. Nature stories tend to arouse his emotions. They put him into moods that are religious. There was a time when all the religion of the world was expressed in nature myth, in crude "why" stories that grew out of the wonder, hope and fear of primitive man. Science began in fiction. Man's imagining about nature was his primitive way of seeking the truth. Throughout its long march from barbarism, the race has been nurtured by nature-stories. They have gone hand in hand with religion. They should go hand in hand with the religious education of the child. The worker in the Sunday school, as well as the mother in the home, needs to be equipped with a fund of nature material.

Primitive nature stories.—The nature stories told to young children should be of two kinds, primitive and modern. In the primitive group are animal stories and nature myths. These are tales that portray early man's imagining about the beasts that were part of his world and those that gave his ideas about the creation, and the forces

concealed within the wind, sunshine, lightning, and
all else that he did not understand.   Tales of this
type should not be told as true stories, but as what
people long ago believed before they came to know
the facts.   Given in this way, these primitive
narratives are still religious stories to the child.
Instead of lessening his faith in the Jehovah of the
Israelites they tend to strengthen it.   They give
him a conception of the handicap of the race when
it was groping and afraid.   Through such stories
comes an added sense of security in the Great
Father whom the child himself serves, and who has
revealed the truth to him.   Wisely presented,
these are of great value in religious education.
Religious moods are awakened in the child as he
sees folk of far away and long ago groping in darkness, seeking God, living in perpetual fear because
they have not found him.   Tales that embody
primitive beliefs as to how the world was made,
why the bear has a short tail, how the leopard got
its spots, why the rattlesnake bites, and kindred
primitive "Why" stories increase the feeling of
kinship between the child and nature and make
him count himself fortunate in knowing the God
who created all things.

The following books are sources of this material:
Nature Myths and Stories for Little Children—
Cooke.

Round the Year in Myth and Song—Holbrook.

Book of Nature Myths—Holbrook.

In Mythland—Beckwith.

Birds in Legend, Fable and Folk Lore—Ingersoll.

Our Wonderful World—Howe.

Modern nature material.—Along with the primi-

tive nature stories should be used many modern
ones, true accounts of animals and plants, of tides,
stars, trees, cliffs, and changing seasons, and numerous other bits of narrative from the great book of
science. Arthur Thompson's *Outline of Science*,
which is in the field of science what Wells' *Outline
of History* is in the field of history, is perhaps the
best foundation book for the worker who has not
time for specialized study. Collections of science
and nature stories intended for children, but which
will be helpful to the teacher whose hours of preparation are limited, are the following:

*Some Useful Animals and What They Do For
Us*—Monteith.

First and Second Science Readers—Nelson.

Children's Book of Stars—Milton.

The Earth and Sky—Holden.

A Hermit's Wild Friends—Walton.

Animal Secrets Told—Brearley.

The Friendly Stars—Martin.

Nature's Garden (Wild Flowers)—Blanchan.

Knowing Birds Through Stories—Brailliar.

Some good elementary biology will also help to
equip the story-teller for his work in giving nature
material to children. Excellent works for this purpose are:

Elementary Biology—Jordan and Jenkins.

The Biology of Man and Other Organisms—Lin-
ville.

Heathen and Christian Epics.—In the age when
the child craves adventure tales the great epics
of the world should be drawn from to supplement
the Bible stories. Rightly presented, these are
religious stories to boys and girls of from ten to

sixteen, exactly as primitive nature myths are religious stories to young children, because they are redolent of the religious beliefs of the peoples among whom they emerged. At the same time children are hearing about Abraham, Isaac, Jacob, Joseph, Moses, Joshua, Daniel and David they should make the acquaintance of Beowulf, Siegfried, Sigurd, and the various other heroes of the epics. They should meet these men first in scattered adventure stories, then as heroes of connected dramas that show a people against a background of religious belief, struggling through the aid of that religion to overcome obstacles and move toward a higher life.

The heathen epics.—The epics that grew among heathen nations, the ones that are crude and barbaric in their elements, such as Beowulf, the Kalevala, and the Scandinavian sagas are especially appealing to children between the ages of ten and fourteen. These stories, when told after the Bible narratives have been heard, and contrasted with those of the people whose guide was Jehovah-jirah, serve to intensify the comfort of Christianity and the insecurity that marked the lives of those who worshiped Beltane, Jove, or Odin.

The following books are among the best of those dealing with the Heathen epics:

The Younger Edda—Anderson.

Sigurd the Volsung—Morris.

Norse Stories from the Eddas—Mabie.

Siegfried and Beowulf—Ragozin.

The Christian epics.—In sharp contrast to the heathen epics and highly valuable in religious training are those that were formed in the several

European lands after the people became Christianized. These are made up of stories of King Arthur and the Round Table Knights, Titurel, Parsifal, and others who contended in the high cause of Christianity. The King Arthur stories, and that of Parsifal are ideal for use in religious work, because they center around the legend of the Holy Grail. During the Dark and Middle ages, the Grail symbolized all that was best in Christianity. They should be presented as the heathen epics are, or as the biblical ones: first as scattered adventure tales in the period when such narratives are craved; later, during the earlier years of adolescence, they should be given in complete form, so that the characters are seen as heroes of a great drama and an idea is obtained of the spiritual struggles of the people who gave them to the world.

Retold epical stories.—In preparing material from the epics, as from the Bible, the best way is to go to the fountain head, to the epical poems and dramas that are sources of the narratives as the world knows them. But the average story-teller has neither the time for this nor access to the versions. Therefore, in most cases, it will be necessary to use some retold rendering of the ancient tales.

Books dealing with the Christian epics in a manner that the narrator will find well suited to his use are the following:

The Boys' King Arthur—Lanier.

Stories of King Arthur and His Knights—Pyle.

King Arthur and His Noble Knights—Macleod.

The Story of Parsival, Mary Sterling Blackwell.

The Story of Sir Galahad—Sterling.

Although the books mentioned that deal with
the story of King Arthur and Parsifal are on the
whole excellent for the story-teller's use, they do
not give enough of the Grail legend for young
people to obtain an understanding of the mediæval
belief concerning it. The story of how the Holy
Grail came to be in the world, and why it disappeared is as follows:

In the crown which sixty angels tendered Lucifer
while he was one of the celestials there were unnumbered marvelous jewels. When he was cast out of
heaven one of these fell upon the earth, and from it
was carved an exquisitely lovely vessel. For ages
upon ages this vessel was somewhere in the world.
Finally it came into the hands of Joseph of
Arimathæa. He gave it to Jesus, and the Master
used it during the Last Supper. On the day of the
crucifixion, Joseph caught a few drops of blood as
it flowed from the Saviour's side. This, the legend
declares, endowed the vessel with marvelous powers.
Whoever looked upon it, even though he were sick,
would never die. Neither would anyone who beheld
it ever grow old or be unfortunate or unhappy.

But after a while the world came to be so wicked
that the Holy Grail disappeared, and nobody had
any idea where it had gone. Then, in the time
when good King Arthur ruled at Camelot, a story
spread among men that if any one were without
sin he might obtain the miraculous cup.

Around this belief of the power of the Grail and
the possibility of regaining it by one without sin
center two of the noblest epics the world knows,
that of King Arthur and of Titurel and his
descendant, Parsifal. Both of these epics are

magnificent spiritual food for adolescent boys and girls. The symbolism of the Grail makes a deep appeal during the years of idealism. An understanding of how belief in it fired men to high deeds is a wholesome influence in any life.

The best retold version of Parsifal in English is Anna Alice Chapin's *Story of Parsifal*. Guerber's *Stories of the Wagner Operas* also gives a clear and excellent rendering of this legend.

Guerber's *Legends of the Middle Ages* (chapter headed "Titurel and the Holy Grail"), also gives facts in the tale.

Other material that grew out of the Christian epics are the stories of Saint George and the Dragon, and those of Roland, Bayard, Ogier the Dane, and other picturesque characters of the time of Charlemagne and the centuries succeeding him. Books dealing with these narratives are:

Seven Champions of Christendom—(St. George and the Dragon)—Matthews.

Page, Esquire, and Knight (Roland, Bayard, Round Table Knights, etc.)—Lansing.

Pilgrim's Progress, Paradise Lost, and Jerusalem Delivered.—A book of books for use in religious training is Bunyan's *Pilgrim's Progress*. At least enough of this story should be told to whet the appetite of young people for the rest of it, so they will read it themselves. The narrator who knows Milton's *Paradise Lost* and Tasso's *Jerusalem Delivered* well enough to recount them to boys and girls in the adolescent years is fortunate. Both are highly appealing and valuable during this period. *Jerusalem Delivered* should be given before the masterpiece of Milton, because it is a great adventure story, yet teeming with idealism. It is understood and enjoyed a little earlier than is *Paradise Lost.*

Historical material.—History offers rich material to the story-teller in the religious field who deals with hero-worshiping boys and girls—especially that part covering the crusades. Many of those who fared to Palestine were not all they should have been, and much crime and lawlessness were perpetrated by them in the name of Christianity. But, on the other hand, there was a splendid company of godly men among them, and these stand as towering examples of all that is fine and heroic. Godfrey of Bouillon, Tancred, and other of the high-souled crusaders should be well known characters to the young. Boys and girls should understand the fervent religious spirit out of which the crusades grew. It is a fine influence in their lives to realize that there was a time in the history of the world when the thought of men was focused more upon religious things than on anything else. The best emotions in these young folk of adolescent years quicken at the thought of the spirit of devotion and sacrifice that led the rich to give their treasured possessions, jewels, gold, and lands, and the poor their few precious coins, sometimes even the clothing from their backs, in order to finance expeditions undertaken for the purpose of rescuing the tomb of Jesus from those who had defiled it.

The Christian martyrs and the heroes of the early Christian Church.—During the adolescent years, young people should also learn something of the heroes of the early Christian Church, the men and women who struggled to keep the faith of

Jesus alive in the world. Hurst's *History of the Christian Church* contains much interesting and inspirational material.

Great Men of the Christian Church—Walker.

The Hebrew Prophets—Champerlin.

The Women of Israel—Grace Aguilar.

Women of the Bible—Henry van Dyke, Lyman Abbot, and others.

Heroines of History—Bristol.

Outlines of the Life of Christ—Sanday.

St. Paul the Man and His Work—Taylor.

St. Paul the Traveler and Roman Citizen—Ramsey.

Great Characters of the Old Testament—Rogers.

Great Characters of the New Testament—Hayes.

The story of Joan of Arc, who through faith in God and her "voices" was able to accomplish what all the mailed knights of France had failed to do, is also of great spiritual value in the adolescent period. Of all books in the English language dealing with the life of Joan of Arc none more graphically and beautifully stresses the religious fervor and patriotism of this peasant girl than does that by Mark Twain. It should be read by every one who expects to tell the story of the pucelle of Domremy who saved France. Another beautiful rendering of the story of Joan of Arc, but far simpler than that of Mark Twain, is the one by Boutet de Monvel. This is especially valuable because of its superb illustrations.

A very valuable book for this period of youth, because of its reverent rendering of the many legends of Jesus that are still told in the East, is *Christ Legends*, by Selma Lagerlof.

Out of the material suggested, the Bible itself

and the various works containing material that has a place in the spiritual development of the child, the story-teller in the religious field can fashion threads of plot and fancy around which the emotions of boys and girls have free play. This play of wholesome emotion will help them as they ripen into richer and more abundant religious life. The preparation necessary to give the material so that it will quicken to the limit of its possibilities the emotional nature of young people and result in worthy action entails hours of reading, and perhaps some sacrifice. But the reward is great. Just as there is no royal road to learning, so there is no easy road to Christian character-building. But the satisfaction that comes with the realization that one is helping to steep souls in reverence and strengthen them in faith, makes all the labor abundantly worth while.

THOUGHT QUESTIONS

1. Why is it necessary for the religious teacher to know something of the Holy Land, its geography, people, and customs?
2. What general knowledge of the geography of Palestine should the Sunday-school teacher have? of its people and customs?
3. What is meant by primitive and modern nature material, and why should the religious teacher be familiar with both?
4. How can the heathen epics be used with profit in religious education?
5. Name some great Christian epics that should be used in religious training.

6. **Explain** the value of historical material in religious education.
7. Name some historical characters that should be introduced in religious work with children in the adventure-loving period; during adolescent years.

CHAPTER X

THE USE OF PICTURES IN STORY-TELLING

REFERENCE has already been made to the value of using pictures in connection with the stories they portray. Pictures help children to see and to understand what they have not seen or may not see in the tale to which they listen. They help to vivify what has been seen, and to heighten interest in the same. They deepen the impressions made. The story of the coming of the Wise Men of the East to Bethlehem with gifts for the infant Jesus is a tale which little children love. If, after they have heard it, they see a copy of Rubens' "Adoration of the Magi," or any other of the great paintings that portray that event, their delight in the story is twofold.

Pictures stimulate feeling, thought and impulse. The child who has seen the "Adoration of the Magi" portrayed by the brush of an artist will not only feel more deeply the story of the Magi than he would feel without it, but he will *think* more concerning it. Impulses similar to those of the Magi will also be stirred. The picture illuminates the story to him and causes it to touch more potently his inner life.

THE USE OF PICTURES IN RELIGIOUS EDUCATION

The leaders of the early Christian Church understood this fact and used art freely to help them in their work. Until the beginning of modern

times, the brush of the painter and the chisel of
the sculptor figured largely as aids in religious
work. Titian, Raphael, Tintoretto, Leonardo da
Vinci, and the other old masters devoted their
genius in the main to embellishing churches, to
coloring canvases and frescoes with biblical subjects
and Madonnas, and to carving out statues of
biblical characters. They devoted their genius to
this work because the church leaders knew that
religious pictures and statues have an emotional
appeal. Such masterpieces put those who behold
them into a receptive mood toward religious themes.
They simplified the task of the priests. Artists
were paid to paint Madonnas and portray biblical
stories, and they gave the best of their genius to it.
This kind of work returned them a livelihood, but,
being on the whole devout Catholics, it brought
them the satisfaction of making contributions to the
church and its work.

Great store of religious pictures.—Because of this
fact, the story-teller in the religious field has a
great wealth of art treasures from which to draw
in illuminating his tales, in making them enjoyable
to his auditors, and in impressing truth deeply.
For the kindergarten tot, the child with his vigorous
imagination, the adventure-loving boy and girl, and
the aspiring adolescent there are pictures almost
without number.

Cheap reproductions of masterpieces.—Cheap
prints of masterpieces are now within the reach of
every one. There are several houses engaged in
making penny, five- and ten-cent small prints, as
well as larger and comparatively low-priced ones
for framing. No child needs to be without the

knowledge, joy, and enriched spiritual life that comes of stories visualized through the aid of pictures.

The appeal of pictures in different periods.— Every great work of art has a meaning for adults, no matter what subject it portrays. In using pictures to supplement story-telling, it will be found that often a painting that delights little people awakens interest and feeling among adolescents also. There is no sharply drawn line of division in classifying pictures according to age levels of experience. Some can be used with value no matter what the age of those with whom one works. Moreover, a picture once understood and enjoyed is never outgrown.

Every picture, however, *when seen for the first time*, during the period of development in which there is spontaneous interest in the truth which it represents, makes a particularly deep impression. When first seen, a painting that portrays a miracle means more in the young wonder-loving child than in the later time when adventure tales are most desired. Likewise a canvas depicting the Queen of Sheba has a deeper meaning during the years of adolescence than in the time when a child wants fairy tales, although the latter thinks it is a very pretty lady. The same rules that hold in the choice of story material for the various age periods apply also in the selection of pictures. Art interest is wider in range than story interest, however. Long after boys and girls have ceased to enjoy the tale of Moses in the rushes, they take pleasure in looking at a picture that portrays the finding of the babe by the daughter of Pharaoh.

A painting of the Transfiguration is deeply appealing to a pupil in the primary department. It has an equally deep appeal during the years of adolescence, although by young people of this age it is differently interpreted than by folk of seven and eight. The teacher or mother needs to apply the principles of story interests in her selection of pictures, in order that she may present the great religious art works of the world at the time they mean *most*, at the time when they will arouse the deepest emotions and noblest impulses. The appended lists are made out with this thought in mind. Some of the pictures recommended for the early years of childhood are suitable also for use during the period of adolescence. If, however, there is any doubt in the narrator's mind about interchanging them, the lists as given can be depended on for pictures of deepest significance during the several specific periods indicated.

PICTURES TO USE WITH STORIES IN THE EARLY YEARS OF CHILDHOOD

Adam and Eve—Dürer.
Adoration of the Magi—Rubens.
The Finding of Moses—Claude Lorrain.
Holy Family—Murillo.
The Marriage of the Virgin—Raphael.
The Flight into Egypt—Van Dyke.
The Nativity—Hofmann.
The Arrival of the Shepherds—Lerolle.
The Sistine Madonna—Raphael.
Madonna of the Chair—Raphael.
Holy Night—Correggio.

The Angelus—Millet.
The Shepherdess—Lerolle.
Holy Family—Raphael.
Adoration of the Magi—Velazquez.
A Little Child Shall Lead Them—Hofmann.
The Infant Samuel—Sir Joshua Reynolds.
Adoration of the Shepherds—Rembrandt.
Adoration of the Magi—Paolo Veronese.
Abraham Receiving the News of Isaac's Birth—
Ꞌenelli.
Ꞇhe Good Shepherd—Plockhorst.
  e Divine Shepherd—Murillo.
     st Blessing Little Children—Plockhorst.
Hꞓ   of the Boy Christ (detail)—Hofmann.
The   ising of Lazarus—Sebastino de Piombo.
The b   hment from Paradise (fresco)—Raphael.
Noah   ling the Ark (fresco)—Raphael.
The Finᴄ   of Moses—Raphael.
The Lost   ᴅ—Soord.

NATURE PIᴄ   ᴇs FOR YOUNG CHILDREN

Brittany Sheep-   ᴠheur.
Shepherd of the Ƒ   ees—Bonheur.
The Sheepfold—Jaᴄ
Feeding the Hens—M
Red Deer of Chillinghaᴍ   Landseer.
Can't You Talk?—Holᴍ
Milking Time—Dupre.
Lions at Home—Bonheur.
Song of the Lark—Breton.
The Horse Fair—Bonheur.
Coming From the Fair—Bonheuᴦ
Monarch of the Glen—Landseer.

In the Primary Department

Easter Morning—Plockhorst.
The First Easter Dawn—Thomson.
Christ Healing the Sick—Schraudolph.
The Miraculous Draught of Fishes—Schraudolph.
Gathering Manna—Dierick Bouts.
Pharaoh's Destruction in the Red Sea—Roselli.
Abraham and the Three Angels (fresco)—Raphael.
Joseph Interprets Pharaoh's Dream (fresco)—Raphael.
Moses at the Burning Bush (fresco)—Raphael.
Destruction of Pharaoh in the Red Sea (fresco)—Raphael.
Moses Strikes the Rock for Water (fresco)—Raphael.
The Israelites Crossing the Jordan (fresco)—Raphael.
The Widow's Son Raised—Von de Brozik.

In the Junior Period

Saint Michael and the Dragon—Guido Reni.
Saint Anthony of Padua—Murillo.
By the Waters of Babylon—Bendeman.
Saul (sculpture)—Michael Angelo.
David (sculpture)—Michael Angelo.
The Story of Joseph (series of frescoes)—Julio Romano.
The Story of Solomon (frescoes)—Pellafrina da Modena.
Saint Jerome and the Lion (sculpture)—Piquer.
Abraham and Melchizedeck—Dierick Bouts.
Isaac Blessing Jacob—Van den Eckhout.
David and Goliath—Nicholas Poussin.

Christ Expelling the Money Changers—Dossa Dossi.

Mourning Over the Body of Moses—Luca Signorelli.

Abraham and Melchizedek (fresco) — Raphael.

Lot's Flight from Sodom (fresco)—Raphael.

Jacob on His Journey (fresco)—Raphael.

Joseph Relating His Dream to His Brothers (fresco)—Raphael.

Joseph is Sold (fresco)—Raphael.

Joseph Interprets Pharoah's Dream (fresco)—Raphael.

Joshua and Eleazer (fresco)—Raphael.

Dividing Israel Among the Twelve Tribes (fresco) —Raphael.

Samuel Anoints David (fresco)—Raphael.

David and Goliath (fresco)—Raphael.

In the Period of Adolescence

Esther Before Ahasuerus—H. Baugkmair.

St. Peter and St. John—Dürer.

St. John in Patmos—Baugkmair.

Simeon and Lazarus—Dürer.

Jesus Teaching in the Temple—Van den Eckhout.

The Entombment—Rembrandt.

The Resurrection—Rembrandt.

The Ascension—Rembrandt.

Moses with Aaron and the two Prophets—Cranach the Elder.

St. Peter and St. Paul—Rubens.

Christ and the Penitents—Rubens.

St. Cecilia—Raphael.

Christ and the Magdalen—Correggio.

Christ Disputing With the Doctors—Paolo Veronese.

Jesus and the Centurion of Capernaum—Paolo Veronese.

John the Baptist—Memling.

St. Barbara—Palma Vecchio.

The Last Communion of St. Jerome—Domenichino.

The Transfiguration—Raphael.

Christ's Entry into Jerusalem—Plockhorst.

The Last Supper—Leonardo da Vinci.

Christ in Gethsemane—Hofmann.

Christ Before Pilate—Munkacsy.

Descent from the Cross—Rubens.

The Holy Women at the Tomb—Plockhorst.

Peter and John Running to the Sepulcher—Burnard.

Christ With Martha and Mary—Le Sueur.

Marriage at Cana—Rottenhammer.

Christ and the Woman of Samaria—Kauffmauch.

Jairus' Daughter—Von Keller.

St. Jerome in the Desert—Cosima Tura.

Christ Appearing to Mary Magdalen After His Resurresction—Titian.

Samson and Delilah—Andrea Mantegna.

Mary Magdalen Laying Aside Her Jewels—Paolo Veronese.

Christ Presented by Pilate to the People—Correggio.

Isaac and Rebecca—Claude Lorraine.

Embarkation of the Queen of Sheba—Lorraine.

Moses Receiving the Law on Mt. Sinai—Cosimo Roselli.

Worship of the Golden Calf—Cosimo Roselli.

Christ's Temptation—Botticelli.
Vocation of Peter and Andrew—Ghirlandajo.
Sermon on the Mount—Roselli.
Christ Giving the Keys to Peter—Perugino.
The Last Supper—Roselli.
Frescoes of the Prophets—Michael Angelo.
  Jeremiah.
  Ezekiel.
  Joel.
  Zacharias.
  Isaiah.
  Daniel.
  Jonah.
Jacob and Rachel at the Well (fresco)—Raphael.
Moses Receiving the Tables of the Law (fresco)—
Raphael.
The Adoration of the Golden Calf (fresco)—
Raphael.
  Moses Breaks the Tables (fresco)—Raphael.
  The Queen of Sheba (fresco)—Raphael.
  Christ (sculpture)—Michael Angelo.
  Vision of Ezekiel—Raphael.
  The Light of the World—Holman Hunt.
Jephtha—Sir John Millais.
Christ the Consoler—Limmerman.

SOURCES OF INEXPENSIVE REPRODUCTIONS

The Brown Pictures, Milton Bradley Co., Spring-
field, Mass.
  Maison Braun et Cie, New York.
  The Perry Pictures, Malden, Mass.
  The Prang Co., New York.
  The University Prints, Boston.

Emery Prints, Brown-Robertson Co., 7 W. 47 St., New York.

Cosmos Picture Co., New York City.

Manz Engraving Co., Chicago.

Scharf Bros., Chicago.

A. W. Elson & Co., Boston.

THOUGHT QUESTIONS

1. Explain the value of using pictures with stories.
2. Why were the old masters so much encouraged and employed by the church?
3. How is it possible to use the pictures of Raphael, Leonardo, etc., in working with children who are far from the great art galleries?
4. In what period does a picture that portrays a miracle make its greatest appeal? One whose characters are animals, children, or mothers?
5. What principles should be applied in the selection of pictures to be used in the various age periods?
6. Name five pictures that illustrate Bible stories appealing to children of kindergarten age; five illustrating stories appealing to the imagination?
7. Name five pictures illustrating stories that appeal to those in the age of hero-worship; ten that illustrate stories appealing to those of adolescent years.

CHAPTER XI

THE STORY-TELLER HERSELF

No matter how thorough and complete the technical preparation for story-telling in the field of religious education may be, the final result depends upon the story-teller herself. Knowledge of the most suitable material and skill in presenting it mean so much that without them there can be no marked success. But these alone do not insure success, any more than a knowledge of legal procedure and a ready flow of language insure distinction as a lawyer. It is the story-teller herself that counts—the personality behind the narration. It is this animated expressive personality that occasions an awakened God-consciousness and desire for high endeavor on the part of those who hear the tales.

The extent of the influence of the story-teller is determined especially by three things—her attitude toward the particular situation, her native equipment, and her personal ideals. These are what make her work alive and vital, and the absence of which renders it mechanical and unnatural. They are what make it an influence for time and eternity, or, lacking them, a bit of entertainment that will neither arouse deep feeling not kindle after-thought. Upon her personal bearing, her original equipment and her ideals, particularly is based her claim to the exalted name of artist—

one who strives to bear to mankind a message he believes it will benefit the world to hear, and who labors devotedly to make himself master of the medium through which the message is to be transmitted.

THE STORY-TELLER'S ATTITUDE

By the story-teller's attitude is meant her bearing toward the work she is attempting to do. Does she respect it? Does she regard it as of great importance in the plan of religious education? Does she believe that through the medium of story-telling she may achieve results difficult or impossible of realization without it? Unless she has a regard for the dignity and importance of story-telling that amounts almost to reverence she cannot be depended upon to achieve the best results. The artist who moves multitudes by his picture, statue, or sonata, is one who believes that music, painting, or sculpture are great and noble arts, and that only he who labors with devotion, and even great sacrifice, is worthy of being a toiler in its ranks.

The story-teller, like the artist, must believe the spoken tale to be a medium through which she can touch all that is best in the heart and mind of the child. Her work must be marked by enthusiasm, sincerity, and belief, or it will carry no conviction. Regardless of what mastery of language and principles of structure she may have, or what her preparation may have been, without these three essential qualifications—sincerity, enthusiasm, and conviction—she will be as a sounding brass and a tinkling cymbal.

Attitude toward the children.—The story-teller's

attitude toward the children is what first of all determines her fitness for the work. In order to be a true educator of children it is necessary not only to have knowledge of the needs of children, but to have intelligent sympathy for them. It is necessary to be able to enjoy good times with children, to laugh with them, to sorrow with them, to listen with interest to a recital of their pleasures and difficulties. It is necessary to be sufficiently young in spirit that one's own childhood is not a remote distance away. Decades may have gone between that time and the present, but in recollection the period of dolls and toy-wagons must be just around the corner. It must be close enough to the here and now that the lights and shadows of the vanished yesterdays are keen and vivid. In other words, though having never wholly outlived the memories of one's own childhood, one must be able to *understand the feelings* of children. One must realize how much the disappointments and hopes of childhood mean, if one is to be sympathetic, intelligently, with children.

Floyd Dell rendered a distinct service to American children several years ago when he wrote his little book entitled *Were You Ever a Child?* By expressing some fundamental truths in a style that is appealing to those who might never read a psychological work, he brought a realization to hundreds of adults of what the sorrows, the disappointments, the hopes and enthusiasms of childhood mean. The griefs of children, the distress over a broken doll, a lost dog, or a promise that is not realized, are just as keen as the sharpest griefs of adults. The feeling of ecstasy that comes with the realization of some fondly cherished dream is almost as tremendous as any rapture mature years can know. Both the pleasures and sorrows of children are too great to be kept by them alone. They want to share both with some one who understands and feels with them.

Children are quick to sense sympathetic understanding, or the lack of it, in their parents and teachers. They comment on it in ways which many adults do not realize. They measure their parents according to other parents and contrast their teachers with the teachers of their playmates. A ten-year old boy who had been promoted to a higher grade was overheard delineating the new teacher to another boy in the following fashion: "Sour, that's her name. Just hates kids. You can make Miss Shelton laugh, but not her. She don't know how. She's terrible old, though," he added, tolerantly, "about seventy-six. I guess that's what's the matter. She's so old she's forgot she used to be a kid."

Except in the years of the teacher the boy was right. She was not fond of children and disliked teaching. She was about the same age as Miss Shelton, her popular colleague. In fact, she was a little younger, about thirty-nine. But Miss Shelton was full of enthusiasm for her work. She loved children and delighted in being identified with childhood. The boys and girls lost sight of her gray hairs, because, no matter what difficulty or problem they brought to her, she gave them sympathetic understanding and help. She had their confidence to such a degree that she could influence them away from some unwise or wrong intention. They felt that she liked them and understood what they really wanted to do.

It is important that the story-teller believe in story-telling as an art that has swayed the impulses and purposes of men down the ages, and appreciate its value as an influence in character-building. There should also be sincerity of purpose—an earnest desire to set the feet of boys and girls in the paths of righteousness—in other words, the spirit of service. But both of these traits are inadequate if intelligent sympathy is lacking.

Attitude toward material.—The story-teller must respect the material she uses. She must regard it, not just as a means of entertainment, but as a wholesome, constructive force. She must believe in its message. The Bible stories and all the other tales she uses must seem to her to be what they really are—truth expressed in concrete form. Without this belief on the part of the narrator toward the tales she gives, the children will detect that something is wrong. If, among the stories designated to be told to her group there is one that, after careful study, she cannot give with sincerity, she should omit that tale. Never, under any circumstances should she give a narrative that is at variance with her own code of conduct or belief. To do so is to have the children feel, "That is what you say, but it is not what you believe." To have this happen is to lose a measure of their confidence, and to diminish the story-teller's influence over them in the future.

In a word, the attitude of the true narrator toward her material is the attitude of the artist. She reveres it as the medium through which she can give a message. To her it is a picture, the presentation of which will inspire to worthy deeds and make possible the abundant life.

THE PERSONAL FACTOR

The people who, upon casual acquaintance, impress us as being of the most force and character are those who are vividly alive, who have abounding energy. We may like the dreamy, silent individuals, or the phlegmatic, slow-moving ones, but they have not the power to influence our actions as the alert, positive persons have. We are more likely to be persuaded by individuals of the keen, alert, vivid type than by those who seem inert, indifferent, and passive. We associate the active, lively, enthusiastic ones with thoughts of success.

Frequently we hear that a man fails in some undertaking because of his personality. He is unsuccessful. He fails to bring about in others the action he desires, whether that action is the purchasing of an article, the investing in some enterprise, the contribution to a charitable or benevolent purpose, or the active approval of his own performance manifested in applause. A passive, noncompelling personality seems to suggest an absence of conviction. He lacks contagion and suggestiveness. Therefore he fails in the realization of his aim.

Many a story-teller has failed because of the personal factor. An unconvincing, colorless personality is just as disastrous to the narrator as to a salesman or orator; a forceful, vigorous, radiant one is an important aid to success. This would be discouraging to many students were it not for the fact that what seems a negative personality to children can be transformed into a positive one. This change does not require an arduous course of training. It requires analysis to determine what makes a personality colorless or compelling. And after analysis it requires close personal observation and eternal vigilance to uproot deep-seated habits and to form new ones. The will to self-improvement is needed.

Enthusiasm characterizes vivid personalities.— To a large degree it is enthusiasm that differentiates the keenly alive, forceful individual from the sluggish, inactive one—enthusiasm for pleasure, for achievement, for people, for all that makes up the essence of life. Enthusiasm is joyous energy, radiating from one possessing abundant belief in oneself and in the worth of what one is doing.

The foundation of enthusiasm and energy is good health. Therefore, whoever aspires to engage in the work of the narrator should be watchful of her physical well-being. Even at the sacrifice of much pleasure she should secure plenty of sleep. Holding an audience in the hollow of one's hand during the recounting of a tale, watching the moods and response of the hearers and working in harmony with them, and at the same time keeping a succession of pictures in the mind, is a nervous strain. In order that one may undergo this strain regularly it is necessary to get enough rest to make buoyant enthusiasm possible. Good health, then, is the corner stone on which to build a vivid and colorful personality.

Enthusiasm versus whole-heartedness.—To put enthusiasm into story-telling means to tell stories in a whole-hearted manner. This one expression, "whole-hearted," should be the slogan of every narrator. Whole-hearted presentation brings whole-hearted response. If children sense the fact that the story-teller is having a good time while she gives a tale, that she enjoys telling it, their pleasure will be the greater. If they do not sense delight on the part of the narrator, they will not give themselves whole-heartedly to the listening.

Whole-hearted story-telling is never colorless and unconvincing. Therefore the guiding precept of every student should be, *Put your whole self into the telling.* Those who observe this rule will not be drab personalities to the children who hear them. They will be met with eager anticipation.

It is imperative that the story-teller be regarded as a vitally alive, joyous person if her effort is to bear fruit.

The voice of the story-teller.—The story-teller must be a pleasing personality. She must appeal agreeably to both the ear and the eye. Her voice should be natural, but it need not be pleasant. If her tones are sharp and rasping or her modulation is defective, she should endeavor to correct them.

In no other way is improvement of the speaking voice made as quickly as by much reading aloud, done with a view to expression and modulation. In fact, oral reading is such an aid even to those who are not handicapped by harsh or rasping tones that it should be a part of the course of training for oral narration.

The elocutionary courses of our grandmothers' days made Americans of an earlier generation more pleasing in their speech than most of us. We are not as much given to "Speak the speech trippingly on the tongue" as they were, largely because we have not had the vocal training that was a part of education in their day. Lip, tongue and pitch exercises were a part of each school reading-lesson fifty years ago. These exercises rounded off the harsh corners and were conducive to flexibility of utterance and beautiful modulation.

In an elocution book published in 1859, this direction is given to students: "Cultivate a habit of reading first in your natural pitch of voice, then in a light whisper, then in a loud whisper. This exercise, if frequently and faithfully practiced, will improve your articulation and increase your control of your breathing organs."

The practice of reading in the natural speaking voice and in a light and heavy whisper has been used recently with excellent results in a university course in story-telling. Several girls whose natural speaking tones were such that improvement in them was urgently needed, were benefited far beyond their expectations by three months of daily practice in oral reading in various pitches. Nor was it an arduous task to them. Half an hour each day was devoted to the reading, and at the end of two weeks, improvement was noticed.

The rule from the old elocution is being used in one of the best dramatic schools of America.

"We get graduates from so-called dramatic schools all over the country," one of the directors of this institution said not long ago, "and almost always we find that their voice training has been defective. Usually we have to start in at the beginning and teach them breath control and modulation."

"Do not all dramatic schools give instruction in modulation and breath control?" he was asked.

"Yes, but they don't go at it in the right way. Most of them try a short-cut route, and there isn't any. In order to get results you have to go back to the old-fashioned elocutionary exercises, speaking in many different pitches, sotto-voice, full voice, etc., practicing sentences composed of alliterative words, and doing a lot of other mechanical things to limber up the tongue and lips."

It is as necessary for the story-teller to have a pleasing voice as for the professional actress. Every student will do well to practice regularly some of the old-fashioned exercises that are considered invaluable in the training of dramatic stars.

Beside reading aloud in various pitches, the following drills for articulation and flexibility of tongue and lips will be helpful:

Read *very distinctly*, and at various rates of speed the following. Let the rates of speed be, first, very slow; then the natural speaking rate. Increase speed at each reading until it is very rapidly done. But *it must be done distinctly:*

Personification,	Discrimination,
Intercommunication,	Interrogatively,
Irresistibility,	Congratulation,
Incomprehensibility,	Perpendicularity,
Recapitulation,	Emphatically,
Metaphorically,	Valetudinarian.

(Short vowels)

Ribble—rabble—robble—rebble—rubble,
Dribble—drabble—drobble—drebble—drubble.

Peter Piper picked a peck,
A peck of pickled peppers.

Ling, lang, lung, long,
Sing, sang, sung, song.

The story-teller's appearance.—The dress of the narrator need not be elaborate, but it must be neat, and it should be as becoming and attractive as possible. Children love a "pretty story-teller"— one who wears attractive clothes. Both girls and boys delight in the attractive garb of a teacher or story-teller, sometimes to such a degree that it affects their conduct. Lads who have been young torments to a teacher who dresses in unrelieved black, and who gave little thought to the arrangement of her hair, have become tractable under the leadership of one who was always charming in manner and attire.

Children are more easily influenced by one who is pleasing to the eye than by one who is not. The mother is loved because she is the mother, regardless of whether she is plainly or beautifully dressed. But give a child his choice between an unattractive and an attractive teacher, and he will choose the latter every time.

Mention has already been made of the effect of a "gypsy" story-teller on a troublesome lad on a playground. In the Sunday school it is hardly practical for the narrator to wear a gypsy costume, but she can wear a biblical costume. She can be a woman of Old Testament times in Palestine, a scribe or Levite, a fisher of the Sea of Galilee, or a gleaner from the Syrian fields. Cheese-cloth, home-colored in order to give the desired effect, will make an inexpensive and effective outfit. Any story-teller who dresses in costume will find a heightened enthusiasm on the part of boys and girls for the story hour. The mother in the home can make an afternoon or evening delightful to her children by costuming for the story period. Beside biblical costumes, mediæval attire may be worn sometimes for a program of epical or racial tales.

A few years ago costuming by story-tellers was almost unheard of, because its effect upon children was not realized. But now that teachers understand how much the appeal to the eye means, story-telling in costume, gypsy, Indian, etc., is a regular feature of social centers where the most successful work is being done. It has the effect of attracting to the story-hour children who might not otherwise be drawn to it. It adds to the delight of those who participate in the period, by heightening the feeling of reality of the Never-Never-Land in which story happenings occur. It is as if somebody has been wafted from that land into the prosaic world in which we dwell, to share with us their marvelous experiences.

THE STORY-TELLER'S IDEALS

The degree in which the story-teller can influence the lives of the boys and girls with whom she works, depends upon the ideals that are incorporated into her own life. She herself must live on a high plane or she cannot induce others to live worthily. Precepts melt into insignificance before the force of example. She may laud exemplary conduct with a tongue of golden eloquence, but unless she prac-

tices what she preaches she will not be an influence
for good.   She must feel loyalty to faith and
principle if she is to inculcate faith and loyalty in
boys and girls.   She must believe what she advocates. The code she establishes for herself must
be worthy, and she must live in conformity with
it.   She must set her aim so high that only through
constant striving can she hope to reach it.   She
must be a person of lofty vision, one who, in endeavoring to know the fulfillment of a dream, is
ever growing.

The story-teller in the field of religious education,
herself, needs to be genuinely religious.   She should
hold the conviction that only through the growth
of spirituality in men, will a world of peace and
brotherhood ever be realized.

If she does believe this, and sees story-telling as
a means of awakening religious feeling and fos-
tering spirituality, she will feel enthusiasm and
reverence for the narrator's art that will make her
an inspiration to those she undertakes to lead.   She
will love the work so much that she will cheerfully
perform any labor that will tend to make her successful as a narrator.   She will strive to become
learned in story lore, so as to have ever at her
command tales that embody spiritual truths.   She
will endeavor to improve her personality and so
become a more pleasing individual.   She will try
to beautify her voice, to enrich her vocabulary
with words that make more graphic and moving
the word-pictures she presents.   She will try to
make herself young in spirit, so that she may be
privileged to win the confidence of young people
and share their hopes and dreams.   All this she

will do, not grudgingly, as the performance of some irksome chore, but buoyantly, joyfully, stimulated by the high ambition to serve in the glorious field of endeavor that has for its aim the realization of the kingdom of God upon the earth.

THOUGHT QUESTIONS

1. What is meant by the story-teller's attitude? Explain what the attitude should be toward the children; toward the material.
2. Why is it necessary for the story-teller to have a forceful, pleasing personality?
3. What differentiates a colorless, negative personality from one that is forceful, vigorous?
4. Can a forceful and pleasing personality be cultivated? How?
5. How is it possible to improve the speaking voice?
6. Why is it necessary for the story-teller to be pleasing in appearance?
7. Explain what should be the story-teller's ideals, and why her life must conform to the ideals she advocates.

HELPFUL BOOKS FOR THE STORY-TELLER

How to Tell Stories to Children—Bryant.
Stories to Tell to Children—Bryant.
For the Story-Teller—Bailey.
Educating by Story-Telling—Cather.
Story-Telling for Teachers of Beginners and Primary Children—Cather.
Good Citizenship Through Story-Telling—Forbes.
Telling Bible Stories—Houghton.
Stories for Every Holiday—Bailey.

Story-Telling, Questioning and Studying—Horne.
Story-Telling in Moral and Religious Education—
    St. John.
Story-Telling in the Home and School—Partridge.
The Teacher as an Artist—Horne.
The Teacher's Philosophy—Hyde.
Education in Religion and Morals—Coe.
Moral Principles in Education—Dewey.
Education for Character—Sharp.
The Use of the Bible in the Education of the Young—
    Raymont.
The Gospel in Art—Bailey.